California
WINE
COUNTRY

By the Editors of Sunset Books and Sunset Magazine

Lane Publishing Co. · Menlo Park, California

Edited by Bob Thompson

Coordinating Editor: Linda J. Selden

Illustrations: Bernice Glenn

Maps: Deborah Neve, Roberta Edwards

ON THE COVERS, California wine country outside and in. The front cover photograph by Clyde Childress is of the harvest season, and the back cover one by Glenn Christiansen is of that later time, after the fermentation has done its remarkable work and made wine out of mere grape juice. The harvest scene is in Korbel vineyards in Sonoma County, and the cellar scene at the Heitz Cellars in St. Helena. It is good fortune that either scene might be repeated with subtle variation in dozens of other locales in the state, north or south.

Editor, Sunset Books: David E. Clark

Twelfth Printing May 1978

Contents

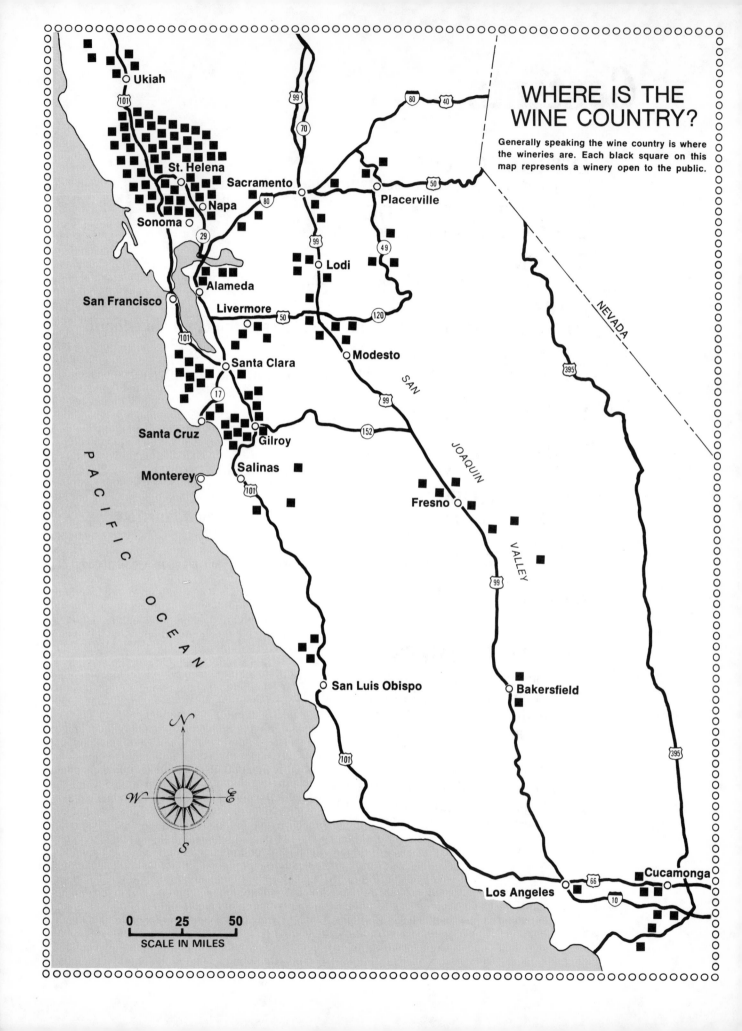

WHERE IS THE WINE COUNTRY?

Generally speaking the wine country is where the wineries are. Each black square on this map represents a winery open to the public.

Ukiah

St. Helena

Sacramento

Placerville

Napa

Sonoma

Lodi

Alameda

Livermore

San Francisco

Santa Clara

Modesto

SAN

Santa Cruz

Gilroy

JOAQUIN

Salinas

Monterey

Fresno

VALLEY

NEVADA

San Luis Obispo

Bakersfield

PACIFIC OCEAN

N

W   E

S

Cucamonga

Los Angeles

0   25   50

SCALE IN MILES

INTRODUCTION

The pleasures of going to see wine where it is made

Touring the wine country is not a new idea. Visitors have been crossing thresholds into California wine cellars for more than two centuries, the official bicentennial having been 1969. The paths are well worn but as inviting as ever.

California's first wineries, adjuncts to the Franciscan missions, were spaced a hard day's ride apart and stretched from San Diego to Sonoma. Junipero Serra and the other founding fathers built 21 missions and established successful vineyards and wineries at most of them. Nearly all of their wine went to sacramental use, but some welcomed neighbors, and some settled the dusty thirst of summer travelers or drove the chill from winter visitors.

The Franciscans abandoned their California winemaking in the 1830s. Others were there to pick it up, so that wineries still stretch along the coast from Pomona to Sonoma. And with time and more grape varieties, the industry has spread a bit farther north and inland over much of the Central Valley. Vineyards have expanded from a few hundred acres to half a million, and annual wine production has increased from a few thousand gallons in the busiest of the mission days to 300 million gallons, products of 300 wineries, in recent years. Production will continue to increase as new wines mature.

California still makes a good deal of sacramental wine. The winemakers, hospitable as ever, continue to cool summer visitors and warm winter ones with the appropriate cup. But it is no longer a hard day's ride from one cellar to the next.

Today, a man with record-setting on his mind could visit as many as 20 cellars in a day if he planned his route with care. But it would be no fun. He would miss all the details, and details are what wine is about.

Through two centuries California has acquired winemakers from every corner of the globe. They have contributed differing notions about how grapes should be grown, how wine should be made, how buildings should appear, and even what kind of dog should stand sentry at the door.

Winery architecture is pleasing to consider in its diversity. During their brief occupation of Fort Ross, the Russians provided something of the model for Korbel's brick tower. The brothers Beringer brought all the ideas for their home from the old family estate on the Rhine. Louis Martini left Italianate pomp behind in favor of a building in which making wine is obviously more important than frills. To complete the mixture, some Irishmen and Finns built wineries to their tastes, and California has exerted indigenous architectural influences, ranging from Mission to Masson.

But, in the end, inner workings are what matter, especially when they are the inner workings of the winemaster's head translated into practical gear. Though variety is spice once more, variety is also bewildering to many a beginner. The thing to remember is that the tour guide will explain why his winery feels one piece of equipment produces better-tasting wine than another.

These days almost every winery separates fresh-picked grapes from their stems with a Garolla-type stemmer-crusher. Paddles revolving inside a perforated drum pop the berries off their stems and break the skins. The berries fall through the holes and are pumped to fermenting tanks. Stems, stray leaves, and dislocated bees blow out through an open end of the cylinder.

Beyond that first stop, though, the visitor may expect methods and equipment to vary greatly from one cellar to the next.

Fermentation of wine is a fairly standard procedure in broad outline. Yeasts acting on natural grape sugar convert it into roughly equal parts of alcohol and carbon dioxide. Red wines ferment in open tanks, white wines in closed tanks. But each winemaker is likely to hold his own view on what particular kind of vessel should be used for this action and in what way.

Many of the other pieces of equipment in a winery have an effect on how the wine finally tastes. Wood-aging cooperage, in particular, differs in its effects both because of relative size and because of the type of wood used, and, not least, because of the lengths of time a wine remains in wood.

Winery touring remains an endlessly fascinating diversion for wine hobbyists because the tastes of wine can be talked about in terms of who uses what to achieve a particular sense of style, and nowhere better than on the spot with someone who helps with the work.

There is no special season in the cellar itself. Things do not move much. This is the serene and slow part of winemaking, compared to the changing world of grapes growing in the vineyards.

The visitor who wants to see exactly how it goes from the start will be rewarded best by visits in September and October, the height of the vintage. He has a little latitude. The earliest harvesting begins late in August. Slow-ripening grapes in the coolest of the vineyard areas may not be ready until early November.

The vintage is a fine time in wine country. The weather just begins to cool after summer's stronger sunshine. Autumn reds and golds creep into the vineyards, competing with the brightness in the clothes of the pickers. Heady aromas of newly fermenting wine fill the air around every winery, and on some fall days, when the weather is just right, fill the air everywhere.

A few districts celebrate local harvest festivals. Organized or not, a festival feeling prevails. Though this is the hurried season, wineries welcome guests and winemakers gladly pause to explain what mysteries are in progress.

After Thanksgiving comes the quiet season. Shorn of their foliage, the gnarled gray stumps of grapevines poke up out of wet grass restored to greenness by November rains. Winemakers, watching the young wines, have only a few visitors in their cool, damp, dark cellars. It is a time for talking at length.

During the vintage season, daytime temperatures reach into the 70s almost every day, regaining such summery levels as the 90s on occasion. Nights get down into the low 40s. But in winter, most vineyard districts likely will have daytime temperatures in the 50s, and frosty nights. This season the tasting rooms serve few

whites but prodigies of Port or something of equally restorative qualities.

March can still be cold, but it is the beginning of new life in the vines, new life in the wildflowers, and new life in weekend motorists. The buds of the new vintage swell and burst into leaf in March, in their annual game of tag with late frosts and hailstorms. The vineyardists disc mustard or whatever cover crop into the soil as green fertilizer and wait for the last frost.

Spring is a tantalizing season for outdoor photographers. The canes remain short on the vines into May, so that vine rows distinguish themselves one from another. Brown earth provides contrast to the bright, almost luminous, yellow green new leaves. (Later in summer canes lengthen, leaves darken, and vineyards tend to photograph like seas of dusty spinach.) Furthermore, spring skies yield the year's best collections of puffy white cumulus and cumulo-nimbus clouds.

Summer, when the sun ripens the grapes and makes the afternoon world all drowsy, brings the greatest number of visitors. It is the season for picnics and touring in general, mainly for those who enjoy company in their wanderings.

As August wears into September, the slow tempo of the wineries begins to pick up until it matches and finally surpasses the tempo of the visitors, and the cycle begins all over again for the 200th time in California and the 6,000th time since Noah got some Muscats going somewhere east of the Mediterranean.

ABOUT THIS BOOK

These explanations will help make *Wine Country* a more useful and reliable guide.

Each map has accompanying tour information for the wineries located within the area shown. The hours listed for each winery are subject to change. In the case of small family wineries, hours may be ignored for one necessity or another on any day. Most wineries close for major holidays.

Abbreviations used in the tour information accompanying the maps may be translated as follows: *IT* (informal tour; in most cases it means no guide or at least no guarantee of one); *GT* (guided tour); and *Ta* (tasting). If picnic areas are provided, they are noted, along with reservation policies.

In the cases of both map entries and main text, the wineries are presented alphabetically rather than in any geographical sequence. Subchapters within main chapters group wineries that are within easy driving range of one another.

Each winery described in the main text has some but never all of its wines listed as part of the description. The listings are in no sense meant as buyer guides or preferences but only as indications of the main focus of production in each case. (In this and in other descriptions we have tried to preserve some discoveries for the visitor.)

HOW WINE IS MADE

From fresh grapes to finished bottle

Although the particulars vary widely from winery to winery, the broad outline of winemaking is always the same and the equipment always identifiable. The illustrations below show in sequence how wine is made.

Stemmer-crushers get most of the juice out of grapes. Nearly all of them in California today are of the Garolla type. Paddles revolve within a perforated steel cylinder, popping the grapes off their stems and breaking the skins as they do so. Broken grapes drop through the perforations. The spindly stems blow out one end of the machine.

Some models are linked to hoppers, so 3-ton or larger gondolas can be emptied in one swoop. Some can also be fed one lug box of grapes at a time.

Presses extract what juice does not run freely after crushing—about 15 percent of the total. There are three basic presses. The traditional type is the basket press, in which grape solids are pressed by a movable end wall into an ever tighter mass. There are both vertical and horizontal models. A second type is the German-developed air-bag press, which has an inflatable neoprene tube inside a perforated horizontal cylinder. The tube presses a thin layer of grapes outward against the cylinder, using relatively light pressure.

The third type is the continuous press, which forces grapes in a steady stream through a narrowing aperture until they are squeezed dry, to fall out the end of the press while still more are loaded into the front of it. (The other types are called batch presses, since they must be loaded, operated, then emptied, rather than being operated continuously.)

White wine grape solids are pressed before fermentation begins. Red wine solids are pressed after fermentation is complete, or nearly so, for reasons described on page 9. Press wines are often kept separate from free-run wines at this point for later blending into wines that will benefit from their more intense characteristics.

Fermentors are the vessels in which grape juice becomes wine. They can be of wood, stainless steel, or concrete. Their capacities range from 50 gallons to 500,000 gallons. No matter what their size, red wine fermentors are open to the air. But because oxygen is a special enemy of white wines, their fermentors are closed to minimize oxidation. (The latter have vents, to allow carbon dioxide to escape.) Most have cooling devices, since the temperature of the fermentation must be controllable to assure desired characteristics in each wine.

Fermentation is the conversion of natural grape sugar into roughly equal parts of alcohol and carbon dioxide

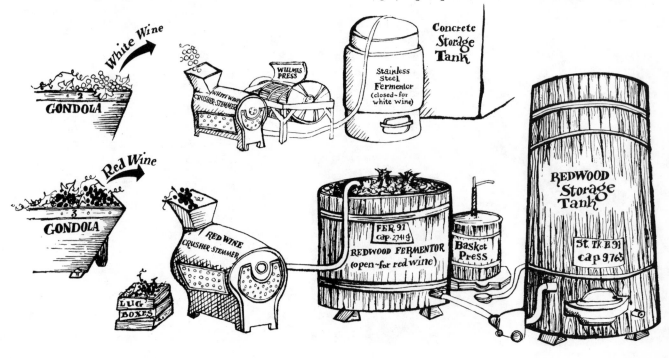

(CO₂). The active agent is yeast. Several strains grow on grape skins in vineyards, but they're unpredictable. Most wineries use selected yeast strains kept in the laboratories from one vintage to the next.

In the case of white wines, juice is separated from the grape solids before it goes into the fermentor. In the case of reds, juice and solids go to the fermentor together, because color and other desired characteristics of red wines extract from the skins as alcohol develops. Rosé wines ferment with the skins for only a few hours, rather than several days.

The major part of the fermentation takes from 1 to 2 weeks. During this time the sugar converts rapidly, and forming CO₂ causes the fermenting juice to froth stormily. When only a small amount of sugar remains, things quiet down, and the new wine is moved to regular storage tanks or casks. There the fermentation may dawdle along for a considerable time. The cooler the temperature, the longer it will go on, unless the wine is chilled so deeply that fermentation stops altogether.

Wine ages in a variety of bulk containers. The collective name is "cooperage." Cooperage, like fermentors, ranges in size from 50 to 500,000 gallons and is made of wood, stainless steel, glass-lined steel, and concrete. The winemaker chooses both size and material to impart extra flavors to a wine or to avoid them. The length of time a wine ages in cooperage also plays a role in this respect.

Steel and concrete tanks are neutral in terms of adding flavor and are usually relatively large.

Large wood tanks, especially ones made of redwood, are nearly but not quite as neutral as steel or concrete.

All table wines start out in large cooperage. Those meant to be drunk in the fruity bloom of their youth are bottled after only a few months in cooperage, usually of a large and neutral sort (though both words are relative, depending on the size of the winery).

At many wineries, wines intended to be held for long aging in the bottle are racked (moved from one container to another) into successively smaller casks until they end up in barrels as small as 50 gallons. This kind of technique requires from 18 months to 3 years, depending upon wine type and winemakers' tastes.

The purpose of racking is to get the wine ever clearer. The purpose of moving some types into smaller and smaller cooperage is to intensify the changes brought on by aging. Most small casks and barrels are of oak. California wineries use American, French, German, and Yugoslav oaks. Each has proponents among winemakers and hobbyists alike.

When the wine is judged mature, it is filtered (or otherwise given a final clarification) and then moved to a holding tank at the bottling line. Bottling may be by hand or by a fully synchronized, nearly automatic line that washes the bottles, fills them, drives the corks (or screws the caps on), labels the bottles fore and aft, and forms a cap on the neck. Some lines are so sophisticated they fill the bottles from the bottom up and draw a vacuum as they apply the cork, all to minimize oxidation in the wine.

After the wine is bottled, it is binned. Binning formerly meant stacking individual bottles in shelves. Now it may mean either that or putting bottles in cases and stacking the cases. The latter method benefits the wine, for it means fewer handlings and better protection from light. The winery may bottle-age wines for a few weeks or months—or even years.

There are variations in the cases of dessert and sparkling wines. See page 86 for notes on dessert wines and page 65 for a description of Champagne making.

SONOMA

Especially historic, wholly Californian, thoroughly vinous

Few counties have more of the character of old California than Sonoma County. The town of Sonoma sprang up around the last of the Franciscan missions in the 1830s. Already the Russians had founded and abandoned coastal Fort Ross.

After Sonoma's mission days, the town served as headquarters for Mariano Vallejo during his term as governor for Mexico. The Bear Flag Revolt, a triggering incident in the union of California with the United States, unfolded on Vallejo's doorstep. Later, Luther Burbank did much of his work in and around Santa Rosa, and Jack London wrote at a home in the hills above the wee town of Glen Ellen.

Wine has been a companion through all these historic episodes, a part of Sonoma from the beginning. The mission had vineyards in the 1830s. Vallejo took them over, along with the rest of the property, and ran a lively competition with Agoston Haraszthy to see who was the better winemaker. (Vallejo's fame is mainly political; Haraszthy is considered the father of winemaking in the state.)

In the years leading up to Prohibition, Sonoma produced more table wine than any other California county. Though it has lost that honor by a wide margin, still the county has 21,000 acres in vines, 34 wineries, and a favored name.

For wine-oriented visitors, the county divides into two sections: the Valley of the Moon, with Sonoma town as its center, and the winding course of the Russian

River from Guerneville all the way to Cloverdale. Healdsburg is the focal point for the latter.

Mendocino County to the north has been an appendage of Sonoma's northern district. Now it shows signs of gaining its own vinous identity. The greater share of its vines flank U.S. Highway 101 on either side of the town of Ukiah.

SONOMA VALLEY

In a world that often is indifferent to such things, Sonoma still clings to its past. The town plaza was the heart of things when Fra José Altimira founded the mission in 1832. It remained the heart when the secular government of Mariano Vallejo supplanted the mission and again when the Bear Flaggers did away with the Mexican regime. It remains the heart of town today.

Time has changed details of the plaza but not its essence. A good many of the adjacent buildings had weathered before California gained statehood in 1850. The square itself remained a patch of bare ground until 1910, when the sizable city hall was built out of handsome local stone. Sheltering trees since have grown up to shade the benches on which townspeople relax in the summer heat.

West and north, Sonoma Creek follows an uncertain course through a string of resort towns. The hot springs that gave rise to the resorts cooled after the 1906 earth-

IMAGE OF SPRING in Sonoma: a skyful of puffy clouds looks down on early green growth in the vines.

quake, and the resorts have suffered slightly reduced patronage through all the years since.

In addition to being a resort row, this was the largest center of grape growing in Sonoma Valley. There are vines still, but in nowhere near the numbers of the late 19th century, when the district had dozens of wineries.

The Wineries

The beginnings of wine growing north of San Francisco took place in the town of Sonoma. Today 10 wineries operate in or near Sonoma. Five welcome visitors freely; the others have restricted visitor schedules. In the latter cases, weekends usually are the best bet.

Buena Vista has endured various fortunes since Agoston Haraszthy founded the winery in 1857.

Haraszthy, the now-a-colonel, now-a-count Hungarian who is widely credited as being the father of the modern California wine industry, set a tone. He brought the first really sizable importations of classic European vines to California, but, because he had unacceptable political affiliations, he never received payment from the state for his effort in its behalf. The hapless Haraszthy disappeared in Nicaragua in 1869, just a few years before phylloxera began to play havoc with his vines.

Haraszthy's sons and others carried on after his departure until the 1906 earthquake severely damaged the winery buildings. Finally, Buena Vista closed its doors. The property did time as a kind of prison farm for

women and was even vacant at intervals until 1943, when newspaperman Frank Bartholomew bought it and started reconditioning the place.

The long-of-memory might have crossed their fingers when they saw the first new vines in very crooked rows. (They were planted by World War II submarine crews on rehabilitation leave, presumably without their navigation officers.) It was not a bad omen, however. Buena Vista has enjoyed prosperous good health since its reopening.

Before Bartholomew sold the winery in 1968, he restored it to something very much like the original. The eucalyptus trees were much taller, and workaday wooden sheds did not reappear on the fronts of the two finely made stone buildings. Otherwise, the tranquility of the 1860s was recaptured intact.

The current owner, Young's Market Co. of Los Angeles, is expanding Buena Vista but not at the expense of the old site. In 1975 the company launched construction of a new fermenting winery near its vineyards on the Sonoma-Napa County line, in the Carneros district. The original stone buildings will serve as aging cellars full of antique oak casks and newer small barrels. (The smaller building has served as the fermenting winery in recent years.)

The larger building houses the tasting room, set in one of three tunnels carved into the sandstone hill. This also is the building in which visitors are permitted to explore at their own pace, with signs and photographs as guides.

SANDSTONE TUNNELS hold Buena Vista casks full of wines, as they have since Haraszthy's time.

Outside, on a slope between the buildings, is a tree-shaded picnic ground. In the warmth of summer, this is the place to have a picnic of French bread from the bakery on the town plaza, fresh fruit from the market next door, cheese from the dairy cater-corner across the square, and wine from the obvious source.

Buena Vista wines include Zinfandel (from a grape possibly imported by the Count himself), Cabernet Sauvignon, Chardonnay, and Gewürztraminer. The winery also offers Ports and Sherries.

Chateau St. Jean, beneath the imposing bulk of Sugarloaf Ridge in Kenwood, made its market debut in 1975.

The new winery, on which construction began in mid-1975, adjoins a superbly proportioned old country manor dating from the era of World War I.

Architecturally, the winery theme is as romantically French as the proprietors can make it, up to and including a mock medieval tower from which visitors will be able to view much of the winemaking process from first step to last.

Vineyards are on the flat in front of the house and on the steep slopes of Sugarloaf Ridge behind the cellars.

The proprietors made wines in 1974 in leased space. The emphasis is on varietal table wines and bottle-fermented sparkling wines. Lots from single vineyards are often bottled separately to emphasize regional distinctions.

Grand Cru Vineyards exemplifies several aspects of wine in contemporary California.

It is one of several wineries located in old cellars restored to use after decades of vacancy. It is one of several partnerships in which scientists form the leadership, bringing with them extremely sophisticated notions about equipment and techniques. And it is a small weekend enterprise, pending prosperity (or retirement of the principals from their original vocations).

Specifically, Grand Cru is located in, on, and alongside the bunkerish old concrete tanks of the LaMoine Cellars, which date to 1886. In 1970 the new proprietors erected a battery of stainless steel fermentors right next to the concrete originals, an instructive sight and, no doubt, a daily source of relief to the cellarmen. The old concrete storage tanks, with doors cut into them, have become surprisingly elegant vaults for the stacks of oak barrels in which Grand Cru wines age.

Tasting goes on in an A-frame cabin perched atop the aging cellars. The proprietors began making only Gewürztraminer and Zinfandel, though each comes in a variety of styles. Other wines are to be added, along with a new building set atop the original fermentors. The new wines were to begin with the harvest of 1975; the new cellars following soon after.

Gundlach-Bundschu was a famous winery name in Sonoma's early history. In 1976 its traditional label re-entered the ranks of the modern-day Sonoma wine community.

Dating from the 1850s Gundlach-Bundschu (founded by Jacob Gundlach in eventual partnership with his son-in-law Charles Bundschu) had a world-wide market for its wines before the 1906 earthquake, Prohibition, and other setbacks closed its doors.

The fifth generation (Jim Bundschu and his brother-in-law John Merritt) began rebuilding on the original site in 1970 and formally opened the winery to the public in the summer of 1976.

Behind the quarried stone facade, the pair has assembled equipment that shows ingenuity and enterprise. Revamped dairy tanks and stainless steel soft drink barrels join refrigerated white wine tanks, redwood tanks, and French oak barrels.

The grapes come from the original vineyards, first planted in 1858, and are made into Sonoma Riesling, Zinfandel, Cabernet Sauvignon, and Kleinburger. The list may expand in time. Current production is small; a neighboring winery buys the remainder of the crop from the 110 acres.

Hacienda Wine Cellars was opened as a new venture in 1973 by Frank Bartholomew, the man who undertook the revival of Buena Vista in the 1940s and who saw it grow too large to be a relaxing retirement hobby.

The tiny new cellar is located at one side of Bartholomew's vineyards, just a stone's throw from Buena Vista. In it Bartholomew makes small amounts of Chardonnay Gewürztraminer, Johannisberg Riesling, Zinfandel, Pinot Noir, and Cabernet Sauvignon from his own grapes and those of an associate in the Alexander Valley.

Hacienda wines are sold alongside selected other Sonoma wines in a finely furnished retail room at one end of the two-story, Spanish style structure. Spacious grounds to one side make a tranquil site for a picnic before or after a tour.

Hanzell Vineyards is the property of Barbara De Brye of London. With Bob Sessions as winemaker, Hanzell continues the revolution launched in the late 1940s by founder James D. Zellerbach.

The notion was and is that California can equal some of the great wines of Burgundy. The architectural statement of intent is a facade copied after that part of the Clos de Vougeot that comes into view at the end of the entrance tunnel. Inside the winery the effort becomes more concrete with a cellar full of barrels made from oak harvested in the forest of Limoges and coopered in Beaune.

But Hanzell is not mere copying. The production is so carefully planned that the crusher can handle exactly as many grapes per hour as are required to fill one stainless steel fermentor with must (new juice), and so on through the whole sequence of winemaking.

A visit is both instructive about thoughtful winery design and a sort of pilgrimage to a place where California wine found a new impetus toward a distinctive style. Hanzell is so small that appointments are required and tasting is not possible. Students of vinous California make the journey gladly to see the place and to buy Chardonnay or Pinot Noir when some of the small annual supply is available.

Kenwood Vineyards, just off State Highway 12 on the south side of Kenwood, seems at first glance to be a typical country winery. Weathered, whitened, board-and-batten buildings snug into a hillside just a few hundred yards east of the highway, behind a vineyard and amid a shading grove of trees, mainly oaks.

It never was quite typical, though, and in recent years has not been country.

The place was built in 1906 by the Pagani Brothers, John and Julius, who were more than typically thoughtful. One example: the big stemmer-crusher rests in a notch cut into a bank between two roads. The proprietors can dump grapes into the crusher without lifting them very high and let stems mound up below, out of the way of work.

Under their proprietorship, this was purely a country winery that sold red and white, mostly in bulk but also in jugs for the local trade.

In 1970 the premises were purchased by a partnership, most of its members also members of a family named Lee. They have slowly altered course in the direction of varietal table wines. The old redwood tanks of the Pagani winery continue in service, but the fermentors are new stainless steel, and a one-time equipment shed has been turned into a barrel aging cellar. Presses and other winemaking equipment also are up-to-the-minute.

The tasting room, decorated with such miscellany as ferns and art nouveau, is in the main cellar. The list of wines focuses on red varietals, especially Cabernet Sauvignon and Zinfandel.

Sebastiani Vineyards anchors the northeast corner of settled Sonoma, starting at Fourth Street East and Spain

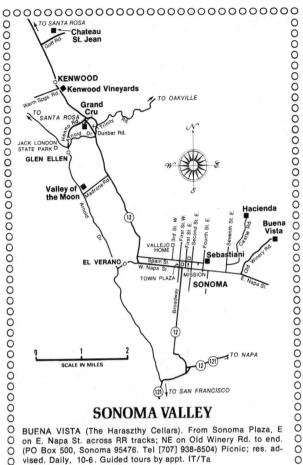

SONOMA VALLEY

BUENA VISTA (The Haraszthy Cellars). From Sonoma Plaza, E on E. Napa St. across RR tracks; NE on Old Winery Rd. to end. (PO Box 500, Sonoma 95476. Tel [707] 938-8504) Picnic; res. advised. Daily, 10-6. Guided tours by appt. IT/Ta

CHATEAU ST. JEAN. N via S.R. 12 from Kenwood; E ½ mi. on Goff Rd. (PO Box 293, Kenwood 95452. Tel [707] 833-4134) Daily, 10-4:30. GT by appt./Ta

GRAND CRU VINEYARDS. N via S.R. 12 from Sonoma 3½ mi.; exit W on Arnold Dr., N on Dunbar Rd., then W on Henno Rd. 1/5 mi.; S on private rd. (No. 1 Vintage Ln., Glen Ellen 95442. Tel [707] 996-8100) Sa, Su, holidays, 10-4. Tours by appt./Ta

GUNDLACH-BUNDSCHU. From Sonoma Plaza, E on E. Napa St., N on Old Winery Rd., E on Lovall Vly. Rd., E on Thornsberry Rd. (PO Box 1, Vineburg 95487. Tel [707] 938-5277) F-Su, 12-5 or by appt. IT/Ta. (Not on map)

HACIENDA WINE CELLARS. From SE corner of Sonoma Plaza, E on E. Napa St., N on 7th St. E., then Castle Rd. to winery gate, continue on private lane. (1000 Vineyard Ln., Sonoma 95476. Tel [707] 938-2244) Picnic. Daily, 9-5. Tours by appt.

HANZELL. (18596 Lomita Ave., Sonoma 95476. Tel [707] 996-3860) Tours by appt. only/No tasting. (Not on map)

KENWOOD VINEYARDS. Opposite Warm Springs Rd. in Kenwood, on E side of S.R. 12. (PO Box 447, Kenwood 95452. Tel [707] 833-5891) Picnic, groups must reserve. Daily, 9-5. Tours by appt./Ta

SEBASTIANI VINEYARDS. From NE corner of Sonoma Plaza, E 3 blocks on E. Spain St., to 4th St. E. (389 Fourth St. E., Sonoma 95476. Tel [707] 938-5532) Daily, 10-5. GT/Ta

VALLEY OF THE MOON. N via S.R. 12 from Sonoma 4 mi.; W on Madrone Rd. ¾ mi. (777 Madrone Rd., Glen Ellen 95442. Tel [707] 996-6941) F-Wed., 10-5. IT/Ta

Z-D WINES. (20735 Burndale Rd., Box 900, Sonoma 95476) Weekends, 10-5 by appt. GT. (Not on map)

KEY: GT (guided tour); IT (informal tour); Ta (tasting).

REDWOOD FOREST in a new guise at Sebastiani.

Street and fanning out in several directions, but mostly northward toward the sharply rising hills.

The main aging cellars, with the tasting room in one corner, are on the east side of Fourth Street, next to the railroad track. In a corner opposite the tasting room, the Sebastiani family has gathered a small crusher, a basket press, and a single 500-gallon oak cask. With this equipment, the first Samuele Sebastiani made his first wine, a Zinfandel, circa 1895. Here is the place to set a perspective for the astonishing changes that have come since then.

From this vantage, orderly rows of varnished, red-hooped redwood tanks extend in an astonishingly long perspective. Behind them is a spanking new fermenting room filled with stainless steel tanks for the white wines. Behind this building, in an open space, are the crushers. Behind them, in a separate building, are the red wine fermentors. Still farther along is an enormous building filled with small oak barrels in which are stored the best of the Sebastiani reds.

Samuele no doubt bottled his early wine at any handy bench and table when he bottled wine at all. Today bottling and case storage require yet a fourth building, across Fourth Street from the others.

In spite of the growth, the sizable collection of small barrels stacked outside the main cellar is not there because the Sebastianis ran out of space within, but because they prefer to bake their Sherry-types with the warmth of the sun.

The tour does not take in all of these points. It would tax the endurance of a Sherpa guide if it did. Rather, it focuses on some of the crucial elements. There is an elevated walkway around the white wine fermentors that gives unobstructable views of the crushers, presses, and fermentors. (Visitors in harvest season can tarry as long as they wish to see how wine begins.) In addition, the tour takes in an encyclopedic collection of cooperage in the main cellar.

Samuele Sebastiani died in 1946, leaving a prosperous but generally anonymous business to his son August. Most of the wines had gone into the world under other labels. In the mid-1950s, August started abandoning that role in favor of having the family name on the family product. That trend continues.

A full range of table, appetizer, and dessert wines is on hand in a tasting room handsomely crafted from old wine tanks. Barbera is a signature among reds, as is Green Hungarian among whites. Gamay Beaujolais is another specialty.

Valley of the Moon winery, owned by the Parducci family (but not the Parduccis of Ukiah), perches on the east bank of Sonoma Creek beneath the spreading branches of an enormous California laurel.

The wooden buildings, some white, some barn red, are at one edge of an expansive series of vineyards.

An amiable management welcomes visitors, leaves them to poke around the winery building for as long as they wish, and conducts tastings in all seasons—but prefers summer because that is the best season to be outdoors in the shade of the big tree. The Valley of the Moon label covers a wide range of generic table wines.

Z-D Wines is yet another of the recent spurt of small, weekend wineries owned by scientists seeking a bit of poetry in their lives.

In this case the poetry is in the work more than in the building, which is a rather humble affair near the village called Vineburg. Precise directions to it come with confirmation of an appointment to visit.

Tasting goes on in the company of an owner, Gino Zepponi or Norman DeLuze, right in the middle of the barrel aging room.

The grapes for Z-D wines come from the nearby Carneros district in Napa County. Most are whites: Johannisberg, Gewürztraminer, and Chardonnay. Pinot Noir and Zinfandel are the reds.

Other Than Wineries

On the old Sonoma Plaza and all around it, visitors may consort with the shades of history. Sonoma's mission on the northeast corner of the plaza is but one part of a complex State Historical Monument. The chapel no longer serves a religious purpose but has been preserved in its original state or nearly so. Other rooms in the lengthy adobe building house collections of memorabilia, including Indian arrowheads, civic documents, mission appointments, and photographs of early fire departments. The building is open daily, 10 A.M. to 5 P.M.

Facing the mission across Spain Street and flanking it to the west, several adobe buildings stand as reminders of pueblo days. Some of these now contain antique shops. Others, within the historical monument, have been restored to demonstrate their original functions.

Several blocks away at Third West and Spain Street, the old Vallejo home has been restored and made a state historical museum. Its name, Lachryma Montis, after a spring on the property, also went on the label for the wines Vallejo made in the mid-1800s.

Many rooms in the old Vallejo house, open daily 10 A.M. to 5 P.M., are filled with the belongings of General Mariano Vallejo and family.

The Sonoma Plaza becomes truly populous only when the town stages the oldest of the state's vintage festivals. It usually comes the last weekend in September, but it may be later, because this is a scrupulously honest vintage festival. Its central event is the Blessing of the Grapes in front of the mission. The blessing is almost always by a Franciscan priest in tribute to the first vineyardists here. In 1967, when a year of curious weather delayed the crop, the festival officers delayed the festival for a week to have ripe grapes from Sonoma vineyards for the blessing.

The town puts considerable emphasis on local history. Many Sonomans allow themselves to be conscripted for on-stage or backstage service in a historical pageant or in one of the parades that celebrate the careers of the mission fathers, the Vallejo family, and the Haraszthys.

There are also outdoor art shows, kiddy parades, a carnival, and other necessaries of a village fete.

The wineries themselves play a quiet role. They elaborate on their daily welcome to visitors but do not invade the serenity of history. The effect is startlingly uncommercial.

Nearby is a memento of much more recent history. It is the old Jack London home, now a state park, on a hillcrest west of Glen Ellen. The turn off State 12 is clearly marked. London, no planter of grapes, did have a fling at growing eucalyptus on a commercial scale. The venture did not work out in a business sense but was botanically successful and left a more fragrant hillside. The house is a joyous tribute to the stonefitter's craft. Within, a museum displays many of London's personal possessions and dozens of his books. It is open daily, 10 A.M. to 5 P.M.

Plotting a Route

Sonoma lies 45 miles north of San Francisco. U.S. 101 across the Golden Gate is the main northward artery. It connects with State 37 just north of Hamilton Air Force Base. That road runs east to an intersection with State 121, which heads north toward Sonoma town. There is one more turn, clearly marked, onto State 12, which runs right into the plaza.

The main approach from the north is State 12, which cuts inland from U.S. 101 at Santa Rosa.

Coming from the east on Interstate Highway 80, turn off onto State 37 at Vallejo. That road runs directly across the desolate north margin of the bay to its intersection with State 121.

All of these roads carry heavy traffic. U.S. 101 is a freeway. The others are two-lane roads, but straight enough for fairly fast driving.

The Sonoma Valley is connected with other parts of the world by unhurried roads, too. These provide scenic if slightly slow access to the Pacific shore on one side and the Napa Valley on the other. Sonoma's handy central location makes it a logical part of many weekend trips north of San Francisco.

On any day of touring both Sonoma and Napa wineries, the back road from Sonoma through Vineburg to State 12-121 offers not only scenery but the opportunity to pick up fresh honey in Vineburg.

Another alternative is the Oakville-Trinity road between Sonoma and State 29 at Oakville on the Napa side. It is a steep-sided set of hills, the Mayacamas range. In either direction the climb is slow and grinding, and the descent is heavy on the brakes. The rewards are superlative panoramas of both valleys and some pleasing smaller views in between. Halfway along is a bridge set with little regard for the needs of automobiles, but the creek that flows beneath it is pretty — and companionable for a mile or so.

A POTLUCK PICNIC IN SONOMA'S COUNTRYSIDE

WEST OF THE WINERIES: tour Marin French Cheese Co., discover Tomales Bay, tailgate picnic.

Sonoma County is a pleasing test of California's capacity for contrast. Its coast, however beautiful, leans toward cool and foggy summers rather than the warm, dry ones of its valleys.

At the expense of 2 or 3 hours' driving in pastoral countryside, a visitor can have a look at winemaking, cheesemaking, and oystering (crabbing or clamming). At the expense of four or five dollars, he can assemble a picnic that combines all the joys of fermentation as company to a main course of seafood.

A well-warmed valley dweller can scoot west from U.S. Highway 101 at Santa Rosa on the Bodega Highway or take a slightly longer route from Sonoma west on State Highway 116 to Petaluma, then west on the Petaluma-Point Reyes Station Road ('D' Street). The latter route has few peers. It is its own pastoral symphony.

In the morning, with the dew still on the grapes, the valleys offer a kind of stillness. Just west of Sonoma, State 116 follows a curving course through dry, spaciously arranged hills, little populated and beginning to warm.

Once Petaluma is behind and the 'D' Street extension begins to be Point Reyes Station Road, the grass is greener and it begins to be dairy country. In the midst of these spacious rolling hills, the Marin French Cheese headquarters come into view. Here, especially if a bottle of wine and a loaf of bread are already aboard, is the place to lay in a stock of cheese and have a look at how it is made. From the cheese company, it is but a short jump after the retreating morning fog to Marshall and one of the Tomales Bay oyster markets.

Wine and cheese are a natural basis for a picnic no matter where the wine road leads. Gather a few sausages and some fruit and nuts a day ahead. Buy the cheese then or plan to stop at a good delicatessen en route to your wine country destination.

What to take? Small individual cutting boards, steak knives (to double as personal cheese and meat knives), wine glasses, and a corkscrew are the only utensils required for this picnic, though a large tray will come in handy.

CHEESE AND SAUSAGE-BOARD PICNIC

Assorted Cheeses: Brie or Camembert, Danish Havarti,

Canadian Black Mountain Cheddar

Sausages: Italian Salami, German Summer Sausage

French Rolls   Soft Butter

Red Peppers   Winesap Apples

Bartlett or Comice Pears

Smoked Almonds   Zinfandel Wine

THE RUSSIAN RIVER VALLEY

From Cloverdale south beyond Healdsburg, the Russian River suffers a period of extreme indecision before it turns west and gets serious about reaching the Pacific.

Its meanderings have created a whole string of hillsides and benches favorable to the growing of fruit, especially apples, plums, and grapes.

U.S. 101 slices straight up the spine of the region, offering a pleasant introduction to the charms of the main valley in less than an hour of driving and also giving direct access to a majority of the region's wineries. But the truly joyous scenery is reserved for those who will dawdle along on the two-lane country roads flanking the highway on either side.

Some of the most impressive vistas of vines are in the Alexander Valley east of U.S. 101, along State 128. To the west of the main highway, Dry Creek Valley offers its vineyards in superbly composed hilly scenes.

The Wineries

The Russian River watershed supports a dizzying admixture of wineries from the gigantic Italian Swiss Colony to the tiny Trentadue.

Traditionally this has been a region for small to middle-size family wineries that sell in bulk to bigger firms with well-advertised labels. Recently the emphasis in the Russian River valley has been shifting toward individual labels and larger, corporation-owned wineries.

This area has become one of the most visitable of the California wine districts. A few of the old penny-saver jug wineries remain, but more and more new wineries play only the varietal wine game.

Cambiaso sits near the top of a round hill in the southeast quarter of Healdsburg at the end of a narrow and twisting lane.

Visitors who remember the place from 1974 or earlier may recall a couple of weathered wood barns and a squat winery covered with corrugated iron, a classic vision of the country jug cellar. It is no longer any such thing.

Today, Cambiaso has a big, ultramodern cellar full of stainless steel fermentors and storage tanks and an equally modern warehouse for bottled wines. The old cellar now holds the wood cooperage, the bottling line, and a retail sales desk.

The winery dates from 1934, when Giovanni and Maria Cambiaso started making wine in one of the wood barns. The expansion followed Cambiaso's sale to the Four Seas Investment Corporation, though the second generation of Cambiaso family members now manages the property for the new owners.

The wine list still has jug generics, but emphasis has shifted over to varietals, notably including Cabernet Sauvignon, Petite Sirah, and Zinfandel.

Because neither the winding lane nor the sloping site permits many visitors at one time, Cambiaso offers neither tours nor tasting, only sales to those who know the route.

Dry Creek Vineyards is, appropriately enough, located in Dry Creek Valley several miles west of Healdsburg.

The small cellar was founded in 1972. Proprietor David Stare completed the first stage of his handsome concrete block building in time for the harvest of 1973. Somewhere in the future is an addition that will cause the place to look a good deal like one of the classic H-shaped wineries of Bordeaux.

Meantime the compact array of steel fermentors outside and oak barrels inside offers an instructive look at an efficient design for small-scale winemaking. It is so efficient, in fact, that the whole tour takes about 10 steps.

Production is not voluminous enough to permit daily tasting, though drop-in visitors are welcome when they want to stop and talk shop. One can write for a reserved place at the proprietor's tasting table, convened on the first Saturday of each month.

Dry Creek offers only varietal table wines, including Chardonnay, Fumé Blanc, Cabernet Sauvignon, and Zinfandel.

Foppiano Wine Company perches directly alongside the old Redwood Highway, not far south of the exit from U.S. 101.

The main building, square faced and wearing a gray brown color on its facade, houses a collection of well-seasoned redwood and oak cooperage. A cottage surrounded by gardens and shaded by trees contains the retail sales area. The roster of table wines includes a vintage-dated Burgundy which often is the pride of the house and a growing list of varietals, most of them red.

Tours are only by appointment; there is no tasting.

The Foppianos are a durable presence in the California wine industry. The original Louis Foppiano bought what had been the Smith Winery on this site in 1894. For most of that time the Foppianos' business has been in bulk wine sales. The family label has been developed primarily since 1970.

Geyser Peak Winery is yet another of those California cellars at once old and new.

As an old cellar, it made both bulk wine and wine vinegar under the ownership of the family Bagnani. Veteran drivers of U.S. 101 through Geyserville may recall the stone and wood facade of the old winery tucked into a hillside north of town and west of the road. They at least may remember the sign saying that no Geyser Peak wine was for sale because the proprietors drank it all.

As a new cellar, a subsidiary of the Jos. Schlitz Brewing Co., Geyser Peak is slightly less and a great deal more. It is slightly less because the vinegar works is gone. It is a great deal more because the original bulk winery

DRY CREEK Vineyards buff cellar building nestles into its site at the foot of rolling Sonoma hills.

SOARING ROOFLINES characterize the cellar buildings of Geyser Peak, expanded in 1974-75.

now secludes itself behind a whole series of new buildings. One holds a vast array of stainless steel fermentors. A second contains an equally vast collection of large aging tanks. Still a third structure has a huge assemblage of barrels and other wood cooperage for final aging of wines that go to market under the names of Geyser Peak, Voltaire, and Summit.

The Geyser Peak label replaces the Voltaire label on the more expensive varietal wines. Summit labels announce less costly generics and varietals.

As a prelude to tasting, visitors can have a look through all producing parts of the winery. There is also a gift shop in the dramatically designed guest hall.

Italian Swiss Colony is here, there, and elsewhere about the state, but its public face is at Asti, near the town of Cloverdale.

Andrea Sbarbaro founded Asti in the early 1880s as a communal refuge for Italian Swiss who were out of work and out of money in San Francisco. The communal idea didn't work out, but Sbarbaro reorganized the winery into a private company and persevered. After Prohibition, the winery and label were revived. Over the years since, Italian Swiss has evolved through several forms and now is a subsidiary of the Heublein Corporation.

It must have been hard to get visitors to Asti in Sbarbaro's time. An inveterate practical joker, he rigged the grounds of his mansion with all kinds of gadgets

modeled after the ones at Hellbrunn Castle in Austria — which is to say that most of them sprinkled or sprayed their victims with abundant water.

The mansion still is there but defused and, what is more, safely off the tour routes just in case some of the old booby traps escaped demolition. The winery, meanwhile, is one of the prime tourist attractions in all the California wine industry.

Italian Swiss (ISC to the trade) sprawls along U.S. 101 in a little pocket valley just east of the roadway. It's an old winery exhibiting many souvenirs of its past, but it also has much to show that is new. In sum, it is as good a place as any to get a line on how wine is made on a large scale.

Tours depart from a chalet-style reception building en route to close-up looks at a modern crushing station, an impressive array of big stainless steel fermentors, and an even more impressive collection of big redwood tanks. Included among the latter is the largest one known, an 80,000-gallon piece with enough room inside to sleep a platoon of infantry.

In the tasting room, hosts offer the full wide range of Italian Swiss Colony wines. This winery has explored the production of flavored wines more thoroughly than any other that offers tasting. They include coffee-flavored, citrus-flavored, fruit-flavored, and lightly spiced wines. There are also several each of generic table, appetizer, and dessert wines of the traditional sorts.

Korbel is a famous name, mainly for Champagnes. The winery was founded in 1862 by a trio of diligent Czech brothers named Korbel. The three of them logged mature redwoods off several hillsides to make room for vineyards. A few of the stumps were too much for them, and these remain today, implacable in the midst of the vine rows. Surviving trees ring the vineyard blocks at Rio Nido, near Guerneville.

First the Korbels and then, since 1954, the Heck brothers have mixed tradition and progress. Much of the basic method used at the winery is little changed from the earliest days of sparkling wine. What is changed is changed slowly. For example, sediment used to be moved down into the neck of each Champagne bottle by means of hand shaking. Now a machine shakes whole batches of bottles at once, but the motion is the same. This is but one of several ingenious devices developed at this winery to retain the old methods in more efficient forms. The tour should be a delight to anyone who has ever taken pleasure in tinkering with machinery, as well as to all who take pleasure from bubbles in wine.

During their tenure the Hecks have added table wines to the production at Korbel. Separate cellars hold the barrels and casks in which these wines age.

Crushers and other working gear are out back. The tour stays for the most part inside the brick main building. Tours start out front at a former Northwestern Pacific Railroad depot, acquired in 1935 for $5 in one of the best deals anyone ever made with a railroad. They end with the tasting of both sparkling and table wines in an elegantly refurbished building that once housed the brandy operation.

Martini & Prati is a winery of few exterior charms. Wooden and concrete block buildings ramble in all directions across a small, rather bare knoll. The major physical distinction is a water tower of great height.

Indoors, however, the firm has a vast array of aged redwood tanks, oak oval casks, and all sorts of other cooperage. The effect is pleasant to see.

The winery dates to the 1880s, including a previous ownership, and to 1902 under the Martini side of its present ownership. Its age explains both its external homeliness and its interior attractions.

In Sonoma County this winery was for years second in size only to Italian Swiss Colony, though a very distant second. Recently, newcomers have dropped it to third or fourth, even as it has continued to grow.

Most of the wine made here goes elsewhere in bulk, but wines sold in jug or bottle under the Martini & Prati label cover a range of types. The Zinfandel and Burgundy are much prized by the proprietors. The company also maintains the Fountain Grove label, which once belonged to the famous winery in Santa Rosa and which now is reserved for the most prestigious varietals made at Martini & Prati.

Only on weekdays is Martini & Prati open for tasting and for tours of the extensive premises.

KORBEL Champagne Cellars were founded in 1862 in the redwood forests of western Sonoma County.

THOUSANDS TASTE at Italian Swiss Colony each month. This is California's busiest winery tour.

OLD CELLARS, *new tasting room combine in harmony at Simi on the northern outskirts of Healdsburg.*

Pastori Winery came into being in 1975 as a full-grown business, partly because wine is a tradition in the Pastori family and partly because the proprietor brought with him stocks he had made in earlier vintages as the winemaster of another cellar.

Frank Pastori's father, Constante, launched a winery near Geyserville in 1914. After Prohibition, Frank grew grapes on the family ranch but did not restart the winery. (He has, however, revived the old bond number, 2960, for his new start.) In recent years he had served as winemaker at the nearby Nervo Winery until it was sold to the Jos. Schlitz Brewing Co.

The old Nervo stocks are part of Pastori's initial inventory in his frame and concrete block cellar north of Geyserville. Most are varietals. All are on hand for tasting, as are the new wines.

J. Pedroncelli is a mile into the rolling hills west of Geyserville on Canyon Road. The wood-frame main winery building, behind a finely crafted facade of redwood, dates from 1904, with additions in 6 separate later years. It is flanked on one side by a masonry cellar full of small barrels and on the other by another masonry building which holds the bottled wines and also the tasting room.

Because the episodic additions have made the winery a bit difficult to walk through, the Pedroncellis do not mind when visitors forego a tour as a prelude to tasting.

The tasting room is separated from the stacked cases of aging wine by a sturdily wrought frame full of French oak barrels. These were brought from Europe in 1967 in time to hold a prized lot of Pinot Noir. Their arrival signaled the Pedroncellis' shift from bulk wines and generics over to a focus on varietals.

The Pedroncelli family has owned the property since 1927. They sold grapes until 1934, made wine in that year, and have made it annually since. The founder was John Pedroncelli, Sr. The present proprietors are his sons, John, Jr. and Jim.

Grapes for Pedroncelli wines come primarily from hilly vineyards adjacent to the winery and a mile or so to the west. The family says it had to give up one block of vines because they couldn't cultivate it after a particularly sure-footed horse died in 1965. The only livestock on the premises now are dogs who have been reduced to barking at tractors for a living.

The list of Pedroncelli wines includes Chardonnay, Gewürztraminer, and Johannisberg Riesling among whites and Cabernet Sauvignon, Pinot Noir, and Zinfandel among reds. The Pedroncellis also offer wines cheerfully identified as Sonoma White, Sonoma Rosé, and Sonoma Red.

Rege Winery caps a small crest about halfway between Asti and Cloverdale in the Dutcher Creek Road cloverleaf. The approach to the winery is complicated not so much by a duck pond as by the ducks themselves, which take a definite proprietary view of the driveway. The winery is a squat, gray building surrounded by sheds and odds and ends of equipment. It is flanked by a frame building housing the tasting room, which is in turn flanked by a bocce ball court.

Rege wines are marketed under the family name, mainly in jugs, most of them in San Francisco's North Beach where the Rege business offices are. It has been like this since the winery's beginning in 1939.

Simi Winery is enjoying a complete renaissance.

After a long heyday in the era before Prohibition and another one just afterward, the place slid slowly but inexorably downhill through the 1950s and 1960s. At the end of the 1960s, the last of the founding Simi family sold to the Russell Green family. The Greens superintended the new start (having grown grapes in the nearby Alexander Valley as a prelude); they sold the winery in 1974 to Scottish & Newcastle Vintners. In 1976 Schieffelin & Co. of New York purchased the completely refurbished Simi.

The Greens reequipped the old stone building with a thoughtful mixture of old and new. In the fermenting room, for example, a long row of temperature-controlled stainless steel tanks for white wines lines one wall. Opposite these vessels, open-topped redwood tanks serve as fermentors for the reds, the only new collection of wood fermentors in the state in any winery of size. A special deck above them is the most useful place to stand during the harvest season in order to contemplate the

RUSSIAN RIVER VALLEY

CAMBIASO. From U.S. 101, Old Redwood Hwy.-Healdsburg Ave. exit, E ¼ mi. to Grant Ave.; E on Grant Ave. to end, continue on lane to end. (1141 Grant Ave., Healdsburg 95448. Tel [707] 433-5508) F-Tu, 10-3. IT

DRY CREEK VINEYARD. From U.S. 101 W on Dry Creek Rd. 2½ mi., then S on Lambert Bridge Rd. (PO Box T, Healdsburg 95448. Tel [707] 433-1000) Daily, 10-5. IT/Ta

L. FOPPIANO. From U.S. 101, Old Redwood Hwy. exit, W ½ mi. (12781 Old Redwood Hwy., Healdsburg 95448. Tel [707] 433-1937) Daily, 9-5. Tours by appt.

GEYSER PEAK. 1 mi. N of Geyserville via U.S. 101. W side of hwy. at Canyon Rd. (Geyserville 95441. Tel [707] 857-3561) Daily, 10-5. GT/Ta

ITALIAN SWISS COLONY. From U.S. 101, Asti exit, E ¼ mi. (PO Box 1, Asti 95413. Tel [707] 894-2541) Daily, 8-6 summer, 8-5 winter. Group picnic by res. GT/Ta

KORBEL. From Santa Rosa, 4 mi. N on U.S. 101 to River Rd. exit, then W 14 mi. (Guerneville 95446. Tel [707] 887-2294) Daily. GT (10:30, 1, 2:30)/Ta

MARTINI & PRATI. From Santa Rosa, W on Guerneville Rd. 7 mi.; N on Laguna Rd. 1.1 mi. (2191 Laguna Rd., Santa Rosa 95401. Tel [707] 823-2404) M-F, 9-4, Sa-Su by appt. IT/Ta

PASTORI WINERY. From U.S. 101, 1 mi. N of Geyserville, Canyon Rd. exit to Asti Rd., then N 1.5 mi. to winery. (23189 Redwood Hwy., Cloverdale 95425. Tel [707] 857-3418) Daily 9-4. Ta

PEDRONCELLI. From U.S. 101, 1 mi. N of Geyserville, W on Canyon Rd. 1 mi. to winery. (1220 Canyon Rd., Geyserville 95441. Tel [707] 857-3619) Daily, 10-5. IT/Ta

REGE. From U.S. 101 S of Cloverdale, Dutcher Creek Rd. exit, W on Dutcher Creek Rd. ½ mi. (26700 Dutcher Creek Rd., Cloverdale 95425) Daily, 10-5. IT

SIMI WINERY. From U.S. 101, Dry Creek Rd. exit E to Healdsburg Ave.; N 1 mi. (PO Box 946, Healdsburg 95448. Tel [707] 433-4276) Picnic. Daily, 10-5. GT/Ta

SONOMA VINEYARDS (Windsor). From U.S. 101, West Windsor exit, W to Old Redwood Hwy., then N 3 mi. to winery. (PO Box 57, Windsor 95429. Tel [707] 433-5545) Daily, 10-5. GT/Ta

SOUVERAIN OF ALEXANDER VALLEY. 3½ mi. N of Healdsburg, W of U.S. 101 via Independence Lane exit. (PO Box 528, Geyserville 95441. Tel [707] 857-3531) Daily, 10-4. GT/Ta

TRENTADUE WINERY. 3½ mi. N of Healdsburg, E via Independence Lane exit ½ mi., then E and S on private lane. (19170 Redwood Hwy., Geyserville 95441. Tel [707] 433-3104) Daily, 10-5. Ta

KEY: *GT (guided tour); IT (informal tour); Ta (tasting).*

SONOMA VINEYARDS cellar building is flanked on one side by a picnic area and outdoor musical stage.

real power of yeast. A red wine in full fermentation has a vigor unimagined by anybody who has not had a chance to see how the affair progresses. This is the closest guaranteed vantage.

The rest of an informative tour takes in a modern crusher, two handsome galleries of small oak barrels, and a fine old cellar full of redwood uprights. The oak, for connoisseurs of fine detail, includes both French barrels and some experimental lots of air-dried American oak.

Since Simi has the only winery tours in California that cross a fully signaled, grade-level crossing of the Southern Pacific railway, these tours are the only ones that ever wait for the afternoon freight to roll through. And most people patiently wait, because of the presence of the tasting room on the opposite side of the tracks from the main winery building.

Simi's wines include most of the familiar varietal table wines, in addition to bottlings of the rare red Carignane and a Rosé from Cabernet Sauvignon. All of the table wines are dominated by Alexander Valley grapes.

The word Montepulciano crops up here and there on the premises. It is the name of the home village of the founders, who emigrated from there to Healdsburg in the 1870s.

Sonoma Vineyards is a sort of vinous Topsy, a winery that just "growed."

The company started as a small tasting room and mail-order business under the name of Tiburon Vintners. Headquarters was an old frame house in the Marin County town of Tiburon. A few successful years later, the company acquired an old winery in the Sonoma County town of Windsor. In 1970 the firm built a striking winery of its own several miles north of the original cellar after adding the Windsor label to the earlier one. The business was still essentially mail order. In 1973 the corporation changed its name to Sonoma Vineyards, having greatly enlarged the size of the winery and the vineyard holdings.

Seven scattered vineyards take advantage of microclimates in the Russian River watershed.

The headquarters winery, alongside the Old Redwood Highway between West Windsor and Healdsburg, is a striking combination of cross and pyramid. The architect was Craig Roland, a disciple of Frank Lloyd Wright.

The functional design was by an engineer named Richard Keith, who set off a revolution with a floor plan in which the working parts radiate out from a central processing core. A good many California wineries are descended from this, the prototype of the system, which reveals itself to visitors from a dramatic tasting room and view gallery suspended among the great roof beams.

The roster of wines limits itself to vintage-dated varietal table wines and sparkling wines. The label, Sonoma Vineyards, is distributed through normal retail outlets. Before it was launched, the wines were available only at the winery or by mail order under the original Tiburon

SONOMA HOP BARNS suggested the basic design of Souverain of Alexander Valley, a new cellar in 1973.

Vintners or the later Windsor Vineyards labels. The latter labels are still available under the same conditions.

Souverain of Alexander Valley has packed a great deal of history into a very short existence, an exemplary demonstration of the speed with which life moves in these modern times.

The winery was founded in 1972 as a sister venture to the already existing Souverain Cellars in the Napa Valley (both cellars belonged to a subsidiary of the Pillsbury Company). Called Ville Fontaine, the company made its wine in the cellar at Rutherford.

In 1973 construction was sufficiently well advanced for the wine to be made at Geyserville, and the name had been changed to Chateau Souverain.

By harvest season, 1974, the building was essentially complete. Shortly after the harvest, the name was changed to Souverain of Alexander Valley. That name goes on, but new owners, North Coast Cellars, took over in 1976.

Souverain of Alexander Valley's sizable cellars are patterned on the old hop barns that dot the north Sonoma countryside. The stark profiles of its twin towers and its sheer size make the building highly visible from U.S. 101, even though it fits into a fold in the west hills.

By design, the building lends itself to tours. Elevated walkways course throughout it, giving clear views of every department from crushers to bottling line.

Each tour group tastes separately from all others in one of four tasting rooms so that the wines may be presented without interruptions. There is even a country inn incorporated into the building so visitors can eat at the relatively remote site.

The focus at Souverain is on varietal table wines. The list includes Johannisberg Riesling, Chardonnay, Colombard, Cabernet Sauvignon, Pinot Noir, Petite Sirah, and Zinfandel.

Trentadue Winery nestles in the middle of its vineyards at the end of a half-mile lane leading east from U.S. 101 between Healdsburg and Geyserville.

Owner Leo Trentadue crushed his first vintage in 1969 and has been expanding slowly since then. By 1972 he had gained enough size to open a tasting room in the upper floor of the concrete building that houses his main aging cellars. Here visitors are welcome to taste Semillon, French Colombard, Sauvignon Vert, Carignane, Petite Sirah, and other table wines while studying the methods of production.

Trentadue sells most of his wine on the spot. He makes only a tiny volume each year, all of it in a time-honored fashion that leans hardly at all on fancy machinery or other sophistications of our technological age.

Miscellaneous Wineries. It is a boom time in northern Sonoma County for vineyards and wineries. Here are some new, some revitalized names for wine buffs to seek out: the Healdsburg area—Alexander Valley Vine-

IT ALL BEGINS WITH VINES IN THE SUN

A grape starts out in spring all acid and no sugar. As it ripens its acid level declines and its sugar level rises.

The winemaker's task is to get the grapes harvested when the ratio of sugar to acid is right. The desired ratio differs from one class of wine to another. Port and other dessert types come from grapes with higher sugar and lower acid than grapes used for red table wines. Champagne, on the other hand, calls for unusually low sugar and very high acid.

In the end it comes down to interactions of climate and grape variety. There is a "right" climate for each variety — or, more precisely, a right range of climate.

California has richly diverse and complicated climate patterns. Vineyardists in the state grow 130 varieties of *Vitis vinifera* in one amount and another. The variables give both vineyardists and fanciers of California wines a good deal to think about.

After a long study, researchers at the University of California at Davis defined five climate zones based on heat summation. (Heat summation is the total number of degree-days above 50° between April 1 and October 31, inclusive. The measuring stick is mean temperature. For example, if the mean temperature was 70° for 5 consecutive days, the summation would be: $70 - 50 = 20 \times 5 = 100$ degree-days.)

The five climate zones:

Region I (2,500 degree-days or fewer). Occurs in Mission San Jose, Napa city, Oakville, San Juan Bautista, Santa Rosa, Saratoga, Sonoma town, as examples.

The university recommends table wine grapes as best suited to the region, especially such varieties as Cabernet Sauvignon, Chardonnay, Sauvignon blanc, and White Riesling.

Region II (2,501-3,000 degree-days). Occurs in Almaden, Evergreen, Glen Ellen, Hollister, Rutherford, St. Helena, and Soledad, as examples. The university recommends table wine grapes for this region also. In both regions, in fact, it recommends nearly all of the grapes used in familiar varietal table wines.

Region III (3,001-3,500 degree-days). Occurs in Asti, Livermore, Pleasanton, Templeton, and Ukiah, as examples. This begins to be the margin between purely table wine country and dessert wine country. The recommended table wine varieties include Barbera, Ruby Cabernet, Sauvignon blanc, and Semillon. The university gives qualified recommendations for many others, depending on specific local conditions. It also recommends a good many of the familiar Muscats and some Sherry and Port grapes, again depending on precisely measured local factors.

Region IV (3,501-4,000 degree-days). Occurs in Acampo, Guasti, Livingston, Lodi, and Modesto, as examples. The balance goes over to dessert wine grapes. Nearly every Muscat, Sherry, and Port grape earns a university recommendation in this region. Among table wine grapes, Emerald Riesling, French Colombard, Barbera, and Ruby Cabernet get clear recommendations. As the presence of Emerald Riesling and Ruby Cabernet indicates, this is a region for which many of the UC hybrid varieties are bred. As the national demand for table wine rises and the university program progresses, this region is turning more and more to making table wine.

Region V (4,001 degree-days or more). Occurs in most of the southern San Joaquin Valley from Madera to Bakersfield and much of the Cucamonga district. All of the Sherry and Port grape varieties carry university recommendations in this region. It likely will always produce a great part of California's dessert wines, but the hybrids and a few other varieties, coupled with advances in vine-training techniques, make table wines a possibility in the warmest of these vineyards.

As the place names used for examples show, the climate regions are not solid blocks but rather dots and islands caused by the effects of hills and inland water on ocean breezes. And even these measurements are generalized. The university has launched a huge new study of climate, based on the old one but going far beyond it. It is likely to be an unending project with accumulated findings published periodically.

yards, Davis Bynum Winery, Hop Kiln Winery, Johnson's of Alexander Valley, Nervo, and Sotoyome; in Forestville—Russian River Vineyards; near Asti—Viña Vista.

On the 1977 horizon are Jade Mountain, Jordan, Lambert Bridge, Mill Creek, Preston and Sausal. Long-time bulk producer Seghesio plans retail facilities in 1977.

Wineries that sell all of their production in bulk do not accept visitors. Some are prominent enough in the landscape to attract attention. These include the Chris Fredson Winery on Dry Creek Road west of Healdsburg and the Sonoma Cooperative at the edge of the village of West Windsor. The Frei Brothers Winery on Dry Creek Road is less obvious but no less private than the others. Two apparent wineries—Sonoma County Cellars in Healdsburg and Soda Rock Winery on Alexander Valley Road—are now defunct.

Other Than Wineries

The Russian River, in its endless tacking back and forth, is a diverse source of entertainment when wine has had its turn.

In winter it is a big and muddy stream whose banks steelhead fishermen populate. With the end of the rainy season it begins to dwindle. In time, in very dry years, it becomes a miles-long series of pools connected only by the merest trickles. Between these extremes of its cycle, the river is popular with canoeists and other boatmen. Beneath the river bridge at Healdsburg, a rental company has dozens of canoes ready for the downstream voyage from that point to Guerneville.

A local park adjacent to the canoe rental emporium provides swimming beaches and picnic sites.

Most of the Russian River resort activity is on to the west, around Guerneville. For the most part it is raucous stuff, tuned to teen-agers who flock to it in summer.

In mid-March the Healdsburg Chamber of Commerce nails up Prune Blossom Tour signs at all the appropriate intersections. The tour covers hilly orchards and flat ones on Dry Creek Road west of town and on State 128 and connecting roads east of it. The latter leg takes in parts of the Alexander Valley, which has emerged as a major new vineyard district since the early 1960s.

The advent of vines has been at a considerable expense to the orchards, but the two remain in handsome proportion to one another. In this season the local vineyardists are just beginning to disc winter cover crops. Only the first leaf buds of the grapevine show. The minute blossoms of the grapes are not due until June.

The town of Healdsburg pays wine a direct tribute each year on a weekend in the first half of May. Then, the town square comes alive with a friendly, low-key wine festival at which tasting of local wines is the main event.

Earlier, during the third week of February, Cloverdale holds one of the oldest fairs in the state. Dating back to 1892, its Citrus Fair is not misnamed. A parallel of ridges has created a frost-free, fog-free microclimate near the town, which as a result enjoys the curious distinction of being the northernmost commercial citrus growing area in the United States. The major aspect of the festival is the elaborate display of oranges and lemons. But it is an all-around village celebration with parades, flower shows, gem shows, and the like.

Santa Rosa, the hub of the area, offers the widest range of accommodations and restaurants. It further recommends itself as a headquarters because it splits the difference between the Valley of the Moon and the northerly reaches of Sonoma County. The former is quickly within reach by way of State 12, the latter by way of U.S. 101. The two roads intersect at Santa Rosa.

Santa Rosa is also the site of Luther Burbank's last home, now a small memorial garden open to visitors. (Though Burbank was a teetotaler, he did his best to improve wine grapes along with other sorts of plants.) The garden is directly across Santa Rosa Avenue from a large municipal picnic park, a few blocks south of the city center.

Plotting a Route

U.S. 101 is the nearly inevitable means of heading into the Russian River basin from either south or north. Moving around within the district does not demand much back road driving, but the scenery encourages it.

State 128 is a particularly engaging road from end to end. From Albion on the Mendocino Coast, it follows the Navarro River inland, runs in dry country to Cloverdale, then joins with U.S. 101 from there south to Geyserville. At Geyserville, State 128 swings inland again before turning south through the Alexander Valley and on to Calistoga in Napa County. Here, State 128 joins State 29 through the heart of the Napa Valley to Rutherford, where it swings east across the hills and into the Central Valley. The road ends at Davis, alongside the campus of the University of California at Davis.

The whole of it makes a fine weekend drive.

The Geyserville-Calistoga leg offers a handy route between Sonoma and Napa counties and an agreeable chance to study the contrasts between wineries in the Napa Valley and those in the Russian River watershed of Sonoma County.

State 12 can be used as a link between Sonoma town and Healdsburg in a similar way, as noted above.

West of U.S. 101, Canyon Road in Geyserville connects with Dry Creek Road, which runs south through rolling hills to an intersection with the freeway at Healdsburg. A few hundred yards south of that point, the Old River Road begins its shambling journey out through orchard and vineyard country to Guerneville. From Guerneville, a lacework of county road rambles through or around such towns as Forestville and Sebastopol. Wineries are left behind at this point, but that can be all right. It's a restful way to meander back to San Francisco.

MENDOCINO COUNTY

For years, Mendocino County vineyards have struggled along in anonymity as a sort of appendage to Sonoma County's wine industry.

Only the Parducci Winery retained any local identity until the opening of the 1970s, when large acreages of new vines brought several new wineries. The major ones are near Ukiah. However, two tiny family wineries are pioneering with wines well to the west, near Philo.

Cresta Blanca holds forth these days in a solid, square-cut building just east of U.S. 101.

The building, having been designed for humbler purposes, as part of a co-op, lacks every architectural frill. Its equipment is right up to the minute, though: stainless steel crushers and fermentors, as well as a cellarful of small oak barrels for the aging of reds.

As a name, Cresta Blanca dates back to the late 1800s when a man named Charles Wetmore founded a winery and made famous wines in Livermore. After Prohibition, the property was bought by Schenley. Later, Cresta Blanca meandered all over the state until it ended up as one corner of the Roma wineries in Fresno. When Guild Wineries and Distilleries acquired Roma, it reestablished Cresta Blanca as an independent label in this new, northerly home.

In the tasting room, visitors find a complete range of table, sparkling, and dessert wines. The essentially home-grown ones, at the outset, include Gamay, Zinfandel, Petite Sirah, and French Colombard. The local list is designed to lengthen with time.

PARDUCCI TOURS permit a refreshing glass before the long walk uphill to the producing winery.

Fetzer Vineyards was founded in 1968 by Bernard Fetzer, a lumberman whose background in the forests led to a handsome set of winery buildings in a handsome corner of Mendocino County known as Redwood Valley.

The Fetzers maintain 120 acres of vineyards in the favorable parts of a canyon that stretches out to 2 miles. From their grapes, along with a few others, they produce Semillon, Sauvignon Blanc, and Chardonnay among whites; Cabernet Sauvignon, Pinot Noir, and Zinfandel among reds. They also have a red called Carmine Carignane, the only wine so named in the state.

Because the winery is small and is also home, it is open to tour only by appointment. However, the tasting room at Hopland welcomes visitors freely.

Parducci Wine Cellars, just on the north side of Ukiah, is the patriarch winery in Mendocino County. Founder Adolph Parducci came to Ukiah in 1931, having launched his first winery in Cloverdale, Sonoma County, in 1916.

Three generations of the Parducci family have had a hand in the steady evolution from country winery to the present one, which concerns itself mostly with varietal wines.

The progress can be measured by the steady expansions of family vineyard holdings. In the early 1960s, they owned about 100 acres. In the mid-1960s they doubled that. In 1972 they acquired another 100 acres, give or take a few. The new plantings are of Chardonnay, Johannisberg Riesling, Pinot Noir, and other varieties.

A white masonry building of graceful proportions first comes into view for visitors to Parducci. Built in 1974, it is the bottling and cased wine storage cellar. The older producing winery nestles into a narrow draw 100 yards or so farther up the hill. It is one of the few small wineries in California that insists on aging wines in large redwood or oak tanks, completely excluding small cooperage. The fermentors in the spick-and-span cellar all are stainless steel.

After an informative tour of all departments, visitors are offered the resulting wines for tasting in a romantically traditional tasting room flanking the bottling and storage cellar.

Weibel Vineyards, the long-time producer of sparkling and other wines at Mission San Jose in Alameda County, established a new producing winery and an attractive tasting room north of Ukiah in 1973.

In time the Weibels plan to add barrel aging cellars to the several banks of steel fermentors. At that point the Mendocino winery will make all Weibel table wines.

Sparkling wines will continue to be made at Mission San Jose. The Ukiah tasting room will be a reminder of them, though — it resembles a Champagne coupe turned upside-down.

〇〇〇〇〇〇〇〇〇〇〇〇〇

To date, the Anderson Valley has only two wineries, both small, family businesses. They are close together on State 128 to the north of Philo.

Edmeades Vineyard dates only to 1971, though the first vines were planted in 1963. It is the property of Deron and Pamela Edmeades.

The winery proper is a small, square, frame building perched on a hillside so steep that the structure rests on stilts. The sales room is farther along the entry drive, where the terrain has flattened out somewhat. Because the annual production is minute, tasting is at the discretion of the proprietor. The list includes Chardonnay, Gewürztraminer, and Cabernet Sauvignon.

Husch Vineyards was bonded by Tony and Gretchen Husch in 1971, when they made wine on the patio behind their house. In 1974 their business had grown enough for them to build a sturdy winery building that holds a shade more than 5,000 gallons of aging wine in upright oak tanks and small barrels. The sales room is directly adjacent in a revitalized one-time granary. One corner of the building is given over to Gretchen Husch's drawings and paintings, the rest to stacked cases of wine.

Husch vineyards roll upslope and down from the winery to the bank of the Navarro River. The varietal wines from there are Chardonnay, Gewürztraminer, Rosé of Pinot Noir, and Pinot Noir.

The production is tiny; it's tastable when the proprietor can spare a bit.

Other Than Wineries

Most of the diversions in Mendocino County other than wineries are outdoorsy and, above all, watery.

In the Ukiah region, manmade Lake Mendocino fills a sizable bowl in the hills northeast of town. The lake has three recreation areas, two accessible from State 20, the road to Lake County, and the third by way of Lake Mendocino Drive from U.S. 101. The lake offers fishing, boating, and swimming. Its shoreside parks offer an abundance of picnic sites.

In Ukiah town a fine municipal park just west of the main business district amplifies the potential for picnics. Scott Street leads to it from the main business route.

The most famous miles of the Mendocino coast begin only a few miles west of the Anderson Valley along State 128. In the other direction along the same road is Boonville, home each September of a first-rate county fair.

Plotting a Route

The highway network serving Mendocino's winegrowing regions is straightforward, even inexorable.

U.S. 101 burrows straight and fast through this part of the Russian River Valley, much of it divided highway. The highway passes close by each of the wineries in the Ukiah region and also gives close approach to Lake Mendocino. No other direct route leads into the region from either north or south.

State 128 departs from U.S. 101 at Cloverdale (lo-

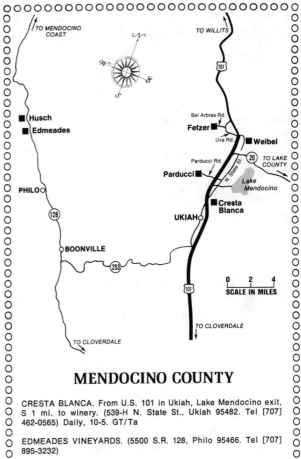

MENDOCINO COUNTY

CRESTA BLANCA. From U.S. 101 in Ukiah, Lake Mendocino exit, S 1 mi. to winery. (539-H N. State St., Ukiah 95482. Tel [707] 462-0565) Daily, 10-5. GT/Ta

EDMEADES VINEYARDS. (5500 S.R. 128, Philo 95466. Tel [707] 895-3232)

FETZER VINEYARDS. From U.S. 101, 8 mi. N of Ukiah, exit W on Uva, 1 mi. on Uva, W on Bel Arbres Rd. ½ mi. to winery. (1150 Bel Arbres Rd., Redwood Valley 95470. Tel [707] 485-8998)

HUSCH VINEYARDS. 5 mi. N of Philo post office via S.R. 128. (PO Box 144, Philo 95466. Tel [707] 895-3216) Daily, 9-5.

PARDUCCI. From U.S. 101, Lake Mendocino exit, E to Old Redwood Hwy., N ½ mi. to Parducci Rd., W to winery. (Rt. 2, Box 572, Ukiah 95482. Tel [707] 462-3828) Daily, 9-6 summer, 9-5 winter. GT/Ta

WEIBEL. 6 mi. N of Ukiah, E side of U.S. 101 at intersection with S.R. 20. (7051 N. State St., Redwood Valley 95470. Tel [707] 485-0321) Daily, 9-6. Ta

KEY: GT (guided tour); IT (informal tour); Ta (tasting).

cated on the northern edge of Sonoma County) and joins State 1 on the coast near Albion. There is no other way to reach the Anderson Valley unless one elects to head west from Ukiah on State 253, which ends at its intersection with State 128 near Boonville.

U.S. 101 is all efficiency. State 128 winds through surpassingly beautiful Coast Ranges hill country at more or less the natural pace of the Model T, which is fast enough considering all the scenery that deserves watching out there. State 253 is a twin.

The only other route that enters the picture is State 20, a winding way to go east or west, to or from the Sacramento Valley.

NAPA VALLEY

Some of the oldest names and prettiest faces in the family of wineries

"The Napa Valley" often is used interchangeably with "The Wine Country" — and not without reason.

A few more than 40 wineries, most of them handsomely traditional, others handsomely contemporary, come at close intervals from Yountville all the way to Calistoga. Many of their names reach far back into the 19th century, and all go into the cellar books of knowledgeable wine hobbyists more often than all but a few in other parts of California.

The cellars in this valley are surrounded by seas of vines, some 20,000 acres of them.

Though neither total is overwhelming by either California or European standards, the appearance of wineries and vineyards is awesome because they approach the physical limits of a small place.

The vineyarded reaches of the Napa Valley may have an occasional peer for beauty in California, but they have no superior. Though the floor of the valley is level and easily negotiable, it never becomes wide enough to lose the imminent sense of tall and consistently rugged hills on either side. What is more, local roads burrow into the heart of the vineyards at some points and climb to panoramic heights at other points, offering visitors the whole gamut of views to admire.

The near end of the valley is just an hour from San Francisco, the far end not quite 2 hours away if one goes nonstop. The essence, though, is not to go nonstop. The distinctions that make the valley worth visiting are lost with too fast a pace.

The Wineries

An old rule of thumb among veteran visitors to California wineries is this: three cellars a day, no more.

If there is any district in California that tempts people to stretch the rule, the Napa Valley is that place because of the simple fact that there are so many wineries and the distances between them are so short. In spite of the temptation, it is wise to resist.

First-time visitors are well advised to schedule tours at one of the larger wineries, one of the smaller ones, and one of the specialists in sparkling wine, and then to come back for further explorations.

Note that most of the many new wineries in the valley are very small indeed. Though the larger ones are able to offer highly developed tour and tasting programs, the small cellars do not have enough hands to do that. Many require appointments to visit, a reasonable condition in any season but especially during the busy times.

Beaulieu Vineyard in Rutherford was founded in 1900 by a newly arrived Frenchman, Georges deLatour. It was continued first by his widow and then by his daughter, who married the eminently French Marquis dePins. The dePins' daughter took a brief part in the management, but in 1969 the two dePins women elected to sell the winery to the Heublein Corporation.

The sale ended the French line of ownership, but already the winery was as international in mien as the new ownership is. The crushers were Garolla types from

BLOSSOMS AND BICYCLES brighten the hearts of spring tourists on a Napa Valley byway.

Valley Foundry in Fresno. The presses were Willmes from Germany, the filters Italian. The cooperage was American stainless steel for fermenting, California redwood and both American and European oak for aging. The new owners have expanded the winery capacity in all departments but without changing the essential nature of the place.

Touring Beaulieu (pronounced bowl-you, more or less) requires some sense of direction. The oldest part of the building dates (under another name) to 1885. Occasional expansion since then (whether it came during the family ownership or the more recent corporate era) has not imposed any rigid order on the whereabouts of walls or equipment. Still, guides tack back and forth with expert ease and cover all departments from crushing station through small barrel aging to bottling.

Although the ivy-covered winery buildings, of cream-colored masonry, are in downtown Rutherford, signs scattered all over the valley proclaim one Beaulieu vineyard after another. (One of the old ironies during the family ownership was that the dePins' daughter was Consul General of Monaco in San Francisco at a time when the winery property was more than twice the size of all Monaco. Since then, the winery acreage has increased from 700 to some 1,300 acres while Monaco has not grown a whit.) Beaulieu, like several other Napa wineries, spreads its vines over a considerable expanse in order to get the best from the valley's extraordinary range of microclimate. (See "It All Begins with Vines in the Sun," page 24.)

The resulting wines include Chardonnay, Johannisberg Riesling, Semillon, Sauvignon Blanc (the latter sweet and labeled Chateau Beaulieu), Cabernet Sauvignon, Gamay Beaujolais, and Pinot Noir. All are vintage dated, as are BV sparkling wines.

They are available for tasting, as selected by the proprietors, in a handsome building at one side of the winery. BV also keeps older vintages on hand at its retail outlet in the same building, from which all tours launch out. BV shows as clearly as any how wine is made on a large scale — by the Napa Valley's measure of size.

Beringer/Los Hermanos winery dates from a modest migration of Germans into the Napa Valley in the mid-19th century.

The enterprise was founded by brothers, Frederick and Joseph Beringer, in 1876, and operated by them and their descendants until 1971, when the family sold to the giant international food products firm Nestlé.

The winery is announced by the Rhine House, originally built by Frederick Beringer as a replica of the Rhenish home he and his brother left behind in Germany. These days it serves as a tasting room.

Uphill from the stone and half-timbered house, about dead level with its slate roof, Beringer's aging cellars include 1,000 feet of celebrated tunnels. The founding brothers employed Chinese laborers to dig them, starting in the winery's inaugural year. They used to be anciently picturesque. Pick marks showed plainly in the vaulted ceilings, which were festooned with dustily black

THE NAPA VALLEY

BEAULIEU VINEYARD. E side S.R. 29 at Rutherford. (Rutherford 94573. Tel [707] 963-2411) Daily, 10-4. GT/Ta

BERINGER/LOS HERMANOS. W side S.R. 29, N limit of St. Helena. (2000 Main St., St. Helena 94574. Tel [707] 963-7115) Daily, 9-4:30. GT/Ta

BURGESS CELLARS. From S.R. 29, 1½ mi. N of St. Helena, E 3 mi. on Deer Park Rd.-Howell Mtn. Rd. Private drive on N side of rd. (PO Box 282, St. Helena 94574. Tel [707] 963-4766) Daily, 10-4. IT

CARNEROS CREEK. From S.R. 12/21 S of Napa, W on Old Sonoma Rd. to Dealy Lane, W 1 mi. (1285 Dealy Ln., Napa 94558. Tel [707] 226-3279) Tours by appt.

CHAPPELLET VINEYARD. (Pritchard Hill, St. Helena 94574.) (Not on map)

CHATEAU CHEVALIER. From S.R. 29 on N side of St. Helena, W 3 blocks on Madrone Ave., N 1 mi. on Spring Mtn. Rd. to winery on W side of road. (3101 Spring Mtn. Rd., St. Helena 94574. Tel [707] 963-2342) Tours by appt.

CHATEAU MONTELENA. N of Calistoga, take Tubbs Lane to private drive, ¼ mi. to winery. (1429 Tubbs Ln., Calistoga 94515. Tel [707] 942-5105) Tours by appt.

THE CHRISTIAN BROTHERS. Mont LaSalle: From S.R. 29 at Napa, W on Redwood Rd. 7 mi. (PO Box 420, Napa 94558. Tel [707] 226-5566) Daily, 10:30-4. GT/Ta
Greystone Cellar: W side of S.R. 29, N limit of St. Helena. (Tel [707] 963-2719) Daily, 10:30-4. GT/Ta

CLOS DU VAL. From Yountville Cross Rd., S on Silverado Trail 3 mi., E on private rd. (5330 Silverado Trail, Napa 94558. Tel [707] 252-6711)

CUVAISON. Just S of Dunaweal Lane, E side of Silverado Trail. (4560 Silverado Trail, Calistoga 94515. Tel [707] 942-6100) Ltd. picnic. Th-Mon, 10-4. GT/Ta

DOMAIN CHANDON. Exit S.R. 29 at Yountville, W on California Dr. (PO Box 2470, Yountville 94599. Tel [707] 944-8844) Visitor facilities scheduled for April, 1977.

FRANCISCAN VINEYARDS. E side S.R. 29, 1½ mi. S of St. Helena at Galleron Rd. (PO Box 407, Rutherford 94573. Tel [707] 963-7111) Daily, 10-6. IT/Ta

FREEMARK ABBEY. E side S.R. 29, 2 mi. N of St. Helena. (PO Box 410, St. Helena 94574. Tel [707] 963-7106) Daily, 11-5. GT (M-F, 11 & 2; Sa, Su, 1:30 & 3:30)

HEITZ CELLARS. E side S.R. 29, ½ mi. S of St. Helena. (436 St. Helena Hwy. S., St. Helena 94574) Daily, 11-4:30. Ta

INGLENOOK. W side S.R. 29 at Rutherford (on private lane). (Rutherford 94573. Tel [707] 963-7182) Daily, 10-5. Ltd. picnic by res. GT/Ta

HANNS KORNELL. From S.R. 29, 5.9 mi. N of St. Helena, E ¼ mi. on Larkmead Ln. (PO Box 249, St. Helena 94574. Tel [707] 963-2334) Daily, 10-4. GT/Ta

CHARLES KRUG. E side of S.R. 29, N limit of St. Helena. (PO Box 191, St. Helena 94574. Tel [707] 963-2761) Picnic, by res. Daily, 10-4. GT/Ta

LOUIS M. MARTINI. E side S.R. 29, ½ mi. S of St. Helena. (PO Box 112, St. Helena 94574. Tel [707] 963-2736) Daily, 10-4. GT/Ta

MAYACAMAS. From S.R. 29 at Napa, W on Redwood Rd.-Mt. Veeder Rd. 8 mi. to Lokoya Rd.; W to pvt. winery rd. (1155 Lokoya Rd., Napa 94558. Tel [707] 224-4030) Tours by appt. (Not on map)

ROBERT MONDAVI. W side S.R. 29 at N limit of Oakville. (7801 St. Helena Hwy., Oakville 94562. Tel [707] 963-7156) Daily, 10-4:30. GT/Ta

JOSEPH PHELPS. From Silverado Trail ½ mi. N of Zinfandel Ln., E on Taplin Rd. ½ mi., then N on private rd. (200 Taplin Rd., St. Helena 94574. Tel [707] 963-2745) GT by appt., M-F.

POPE VALLEY. From S.R. 29, E 11 mi. on Deer Pk.-Howell Mt. Rd., left 2 mi. on Pope Valley Rd. (6613 Pope Valley Rd., Pope Valley 94567. Tel [707] 965-2192) Picnic. M-F, 12-5; Sa, Su, 9-6. Ta

V. SATTUI. E side of S.R. 29, ½ mi. S of St. Helena at White Lane. (St. Helena Hwy. S., St. Helena 94574. Tel [707] 963-7774) Picnic. June-Oct. Daily, 10-6; Nov.-May W-M, 10-5:30. Ta

SCHRAMSBERG. From S.R. 29, 6 mi. N of St. Helena, W off hwy. on pvt. rd. (Calistoga 94515. Tel [707] 942-4558) Tours by appt., W-Su.

SPRING MOUNTAIN VINEYARDS. From S.R. 29 on N side of St. Helena, W 3 blocks on Madrone Ave., N ½ mi. to pvt. rd. (2805 Spring Mtn. Rd., St. Helena 94574. Tel [707] 963-4341) Tours by appt. only.

STAG'S LEAP WINE CELLAR. From Yountville Cross Rd. S on Silverado Trail 2.2 mi. E side of hwy. (5766 Silverado Trail, Napa 94558. Tel [707] 944-2782) Tours by appt.

STERLING VINEYARDS. From S.R. 29, 7 mi. N of St. Helena, E ½ mi. on Dunaweal, S to parking lot. (1111 Dunaweal Ln., Calistoga 94515. Tel [707] 942-5151) Daily, 10:30-4:30. IT/Ta

STONEGATE. From S.R. 29, 7 mi. N of St. Helena, E ⅛ mi. on Dunaweal, S side of rd. (1183 Dunaweal Ln., Calistoga 94515. Tel [707] 942-6500)

STONY HILL. (PO Box 308, St. Helena 94574.) Tours by written appt. (Not on map)

SUTTER HOME. W side S.R. 29 ½ mi. S of St. Helena. (277 St. Helena Hwy. S., St. Helena 94574. Tel [707] 963-3104) Daily, 9:30-5. Ta

VILLA MT. EDEN. N side Oakville Cross Rd. near Silverado Trail. (Mt. Eden Ranch, Oakville 94562. Tel [707] 944-8431) Weekdays by appt.

WINERIES OUTSIDE OF MAP AREA

NICHELINI. From S.R. 29 at Rutherford, E 11 mi. on S.R. 128. (2349 Lower Chiles Rd., St. Helena 94574. Tel [707] 963-3357) Ltd. picnic. Sa, Su, holidays, 10-6. Ta (Not on map)

KEY: GT (guided tour); IT (informal tour); Ta (tasting).

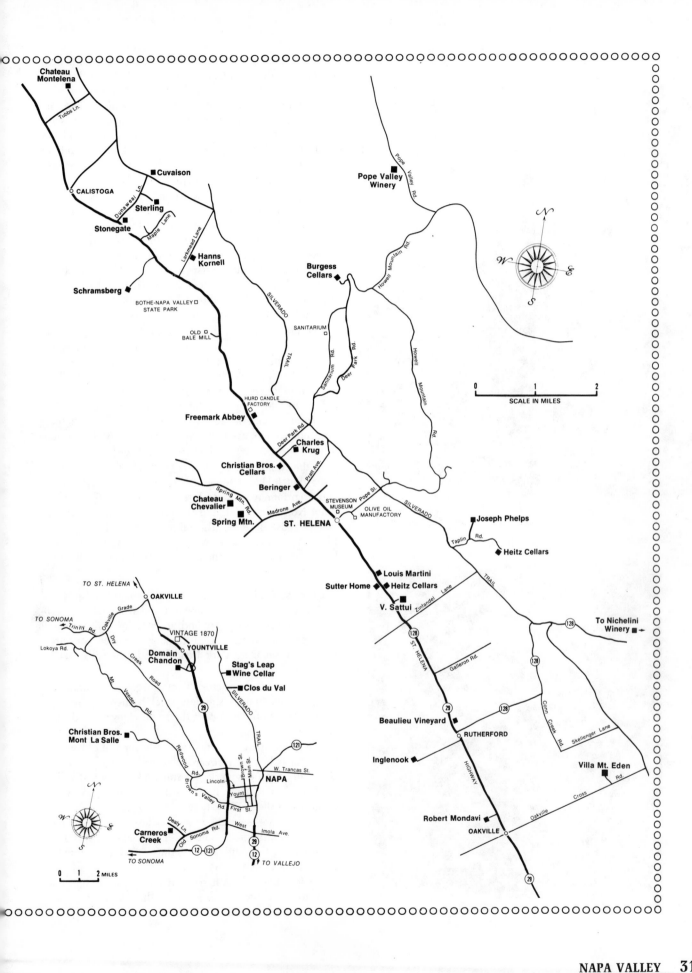

RHINE HOUSE and palm tree at Beringer winery symbolize the ties between Europe and California.

lichen. (Some of the guides set great store by the lichen, claiming it did wonders for the wine. Science disputed with them.) Once the roof developed a tendency to drop chunks of stone onto workers and visitors alike, the new proprietors lined the whole crisscrossing gallery with gray gunite. As a result the place looks a bit like a Hollywood movie set, but nobody gets skulled by falling rock any more, and the wines age as well as they ever did in a fine collection of oak puncheons.

The stone building that fronts the tunnels holds a sizable collection of big, upright redwood tanks and several old casks with heads carved by German master carvers. The tour does not go onto the second story of the building, which only holds more puncheons, but, as proper credit to the craftsmen who built the structure, observe that the upper floor is deck-laid and so watertight after nearly a century of service that it still could be flooded for washing.

Beringer expanded greatly in the last decades of the family ownership and has grown a good deal more since Nestlé acquired it. The enterprise has long since outgrown the old tunnels and stone building. Now all of the crushing and fermenting and a fair proportion of aging are done across the highway from the Rhine House in a modern facility dating from 1974. The tour does not encompass that part of the winery, but a film in the visitor center explains what goes on there.

In the Rhine House, visitors taste selected wines from a list that includes Johannisberg Riesling, Fumé Blanc, and Chardonnay among whites and Cabernet Sauvignon, Pinot Noir, Zinfandel, and the house special, Barenblut, among reds. Beringer also offers Sherries, Ports, and a Malvasia Bianca. The winery maintains a secondary label, Los Hermanos, for table wines less costly than its Beringer line.

Burgess Cellars emerged as a new name in the Napa Valley in 1972, but the vineyard and winery have been around for decades. To find it, veteran visitors need only go where they used to look for Lee Stewart's Souverain, on Deer Park Road high in the hills east of St. Helena.

The present proprietor, Tom Burgess, has added a modest collection of stainless steel fermentors but has otherwise maintained intact the small vineyard and winery Stewart developed.

It is a fine place to visit, not only for the old woodframe cellar but for vineyards that roll from a high ridge downhill past the winery to a small lake almost at valley floor level. The view northward takes in an awesome expanse of valley to Calistoga.

There is not enough wine to allow regular tasting, but the proprietor or one of his cellarmen will lead visitors on a thorough tour of the winery from crusher to retail sales room.

Picnic tables beneath trees at one edge of the vineyard are available for use, though their popularity suggests reserving well ahead of a visit.

BEAULIEU'S main cellar just alongside State 29.

Carneros Creek, founded in 1973, snugs into a hidden fold of the Carneros district south of Napa City, in a small, pleasantly understated, rectangular building.

Stainless steel fermentors occupy a roofed shed at the rear; the barrel aging cellar takes up the majority of floor space inside the masonry block walls. Visitors are welcomed within a small office and laboratory in one corner.

When work does not demand undivided attention, someone — probably Francis Mahoney or one of the other owning partners — gladly will stop to talk shop with casual visitors. An appointment assures time to go into detail about the source vineyards or the style of the wines. There is no tasting, for lack of size, but the short list of wines — Chardonnay, Chenin Blanc, Cabernet Sauvignon, Pinot Noir, and Zinfandel — is available for retail sale.

Chappellet Vineyard perches on a lofty slope above Lake Hennessey and is certainly one of the most dramatic of California wine estates.

The property east of Rutherford is so imposing, in fact, that owner Donn Chappellet could afford to underplay the winery he had built in 1969. In the shape of a pyramid, it nestles into its slope at the bottom corner of a vineyard block. The sloping walls are of earth-tone oxidized metal sheathing. Earth mounds up against the bases as a gesture toward integration into the site.

Within, however, the cathedral-like dimensions of the building assert themselves, an impression aided by natural wood finishing. The roof soars to its peak above three triangular work areas — stainless steel fermentors on one side, small barrels on the second, and bottled wines on the third.

There is no tour and no tasting, only retail sales by appointment of Chardonnay, Chenin Blanc, Johannisberg Riesling, and Cabernet Sauvignon.

Chateau Chevalier revives one of the Napa Valley's more flamboyant bits of 19th century winery architecture.

An aggressive businessman named F. Chevalier had erected the towered and turreted stone building on its steep hillside in 1891. He called the place Chateau Chevalier. In it he produced Castle brand wines.

After a long hiatus, the old building became a winery once again in 1969, though on a smaller scale than originally. The upper stories had been transformed into a residence during the property's nonvinous days and now are occupied by the family of managing partner Greg Bisonnette. Only the lowest cellar holds wine.

The firm makes wines under two labels. Those called Chateau Chevalier come from the sharply sloping home vineyards owned by James E. Frew in a kind of joint venture. Wines called Mountainside are from grapes purchased from independent growers.

Even with the added grapes from other vineyards, production is so small that tasting is at the proprietor's discretion. All who wish to visit, however, are welcome if they call or write ahead for an appointment.

ROLLING WAVES of vines at the novitiate and winery of The Christian Brothers at Mont LaSalle.

CARVED DOORS lead to the aging cellars at Burgess.

ROUND ARCHES and red tile roof of Spanish colonial architecture characterize the winery called Cuvaison.

Chateau Montelena is both a new winery and an old one in the Napa Valley.

The finely crafted stone building dates back to the 1800s, when Alfred A. Tubbs had it built on its hilly site north of Calistoga just where the road to Lake County begins to bend up over one shoulder of Mt. St. Helena.

In its present form, dating from 1969, the winery borrows one of the label names from the pre-Prohibition Tubbs days, but otherwise is a modern, efficient example of a small, estatelike property. Within the old stone walls, one half of the main cellar holds stainless steel fermentors; the other half is devoted to row upon row of oak barrels from all over Europe, and one row of ovals from Germany. A flanking room contains the bottling line and bottled wines.

During the long interval between Tubbs's proprietorship and the current one, one owner, named Yort Frank, began to make the property into a showcase Chinese garden. His legacy — a lake with tea houses on islands — makes a serene setting for picnics. It is available only to wine-oriented clubs, which may reserve the grounds for weekend dates. Individual visitors must make appointments to come on weekdays and be content with a strolling tour of winery and grounds. The picnic areas are not open then.

Chateau Montelena has but four wines on its list: Chardonnay and Johannisberg Riesling in whites, and Cabernet Sauvignon and Zinfandel in reds. They can be purchased on the premises, but the supply is too short for tasting.

The Christian Brothers began their California wine-making in Martinez shortly before the turn of the century. A bas-relief in the winery office at Mont LaSalle shows one of the brothers at Martinez crushing grapes in a horse trough with a wooden club.

By the time the Christian Brothers packed up to come to the Napa Valley in 1930, the equipment they barged across San Francisco Bay was much improved over the trough and club. Now their winery operations are the largest in Napa, far-flung, and a dazzling mixture of the traditional and the technically advanced.

Headquarters is at Mont LaSalle, west of Napa City and just below the Mayacamas Mountains' ridge tops. In the midst of 200 acres of rolling vineyard, a winery and a novitiate stand side by side against a backdrop of thickly wooded hills. The winery is the older building. A traditional stone barn, it was built in 1903 by Theodore Gier, whose pre-Prohibition Giersberger Rhine was a critical success in its time. The original home of the Brothers in Napa, this winery now serves only as an aging cellar, its two stories filled with both old and new oak. The old uprights on the ground floor were Gier's fermenting tanks at the turn of the century.

The novitiate, of diverse materials, is the more imposing structure, following the architectural tradition of the church which this winery serves (both by producing sacramental wines and producing revenue to operate the schools of The Christian Brothers).

The novitiate is a training ground for future members of the order and is kept private.

The other aging cellar in the valley is a good deal

larger than the Gier place. It is the monumental Greystone Cellars at the northern edge of St. Helena. Greystone dates from 1888, when William Bowers Bourn used a small part of his great fortune to build the vast stone building. The Christian Brothers bought the property in 1950 when their stock of aging wines grew too great for Mont LaSalle to hold.

There are tours of both Greystone and Mont LaSalle and tasting at both cellars. Greystone has, as a bonus attraction, some of Brother Timothy's seemingly limitless corkscrew collection.

Crushing, fermenting, and bottling are all done at the workaday South St. Helena winery, its big, ultramodern fermenting installation visible from State Highway 29 but not open to visit.

At the two tasting rooms, nearly all of The Christian Brothers' long list of wines is available for sampling. The list includes several estate bottlings from selected vineyards. Of special pride are the Pineau de la Loire and Napa Fumé among whites, and the Pinot St. George among reds. A specialty is a light, sweet Muscat called Chateau LaSalle.

The Brothers close the wineries to tours on Good Friday, Easter, Thanksgiving, Christmas, and New Year's Day.

Clos du Val, an altogether new winery at its founding in 1972, comes by its French name honestly, for the principal owner and the winemaker both are French.

The winery building, elegantly proportioned and handsome in an understated, almost plain-faced way, occupies a square cut into one corner of the Chimney Rock Golf Course on the Silverado Trail.

At present it is not organized for visitors beyond retail sales of its only two wines: Cabernet Sauvignon and Zinfandel. (A walk through would show two rows of stainless steel fermentors, a double row of small tanks of Slavic oak, and several ranks of European oak barrels.)

Cuvaison, Inc., houses itself in a Spanish colonial-style building on the Silverado Trail not far from Calistoga, at the north end of the Napa Valley.

New owners, a company called CT Corporation System, spent most of 1973-74 changing the winery from a small, countrified operation into one of substance.

Cuvaison's original owner, Thomas Cottrell, with a partner, launched the winery in 1971 in something that looked suspiciously like a Depression-era hunting shack. A twin row of stainless steel fermentors a hundred yards to the rear were the impressive structures on the site.

Now the fermentors hide behind the finely made main cellar, and the first building — much rebuilt — houses the tasting room. All hands may taste Cuvaison varietal wines. Groups may tour the cellar after arranging in advance.

Franciscan Winery has had difficult beginnings since its founding in 1971. The buildings, alongside State 29 between Rutherford and St. Helena, were anonymous for several years. The only visible sign that they housed

a winery was the battery of fermenting tanks alongside the north wall.

However, new owners in 1975 put the name out front and opened Franciscan to tours and tasting for the first time in its short history. The new proprietors, partners, are a Colorado businessman named Raymond T. Duncan, and Justin Meyer, a veteran hand in Napa Valley winemaking.

A tour of Franciscan takes in all phases from crushers to bottling line, including the stainless steel fermentors and the aging cellars full of redwood and oak tanks and casks. Tasting in the spacious visitor hall ranges across most of the familiar varietals under the Franciscan label. The firm also maintains a less costly second label, Friars Table, for its generics and jugs.

Freemark Abbey, when the firm was founded in 1967, revived an older label and a still older winery building.

The original label dated from 1939 and endured into the early 1960s. (There was no particular religious affiliation. The name derived from the Free in Charles Freeman, the Mark in Mark Foster, and the Abbey which was a nickname of Albert Ahern — this trio was the original partnership.) Seeing no way to improve on the original name, the partnership of seven new owners applied it to a new generation of wines that includes Chardonnay, Johannisberg Riesling, Cabernet Sauvignon, Pinot Noir, and Petite Sirah. Edelwein, a botrytised white wine, is made when conditions are right.

The current owners have been required to improve upon the building in which they launched their winery. After the demise of the original Freemark Abbey, the fine old stone cellars built in the 1880s as the Lombarda Winery had been turned into a collection of specialty shops.

The new Freemark Abbey had to crowd itself into the lower story, less than half the original space. In 1973, weary of going everywhere sideways, the partners built a new structure alongside the old one to house the bottling and cased wine storage.

Tours begin in the new building in a room furnished to break an antique collector's heart. They go first into the original cellars (where stainless steel fermentors and oak barrels are so closely packed that visitors must go single file) and then back to the bottling room in the new building.

There is no tasting of Freemark Abbey wines on the premises, only retail sales.

Heitz Cellars comes in two parts. The original winery building now is the tasting room and a supplementary aging cellar. It is a small, redwood-faced structure on the St. Helena Highway just south of town. Joe Heitz's present producing winery is tucked away east of St. Helena and the Silverado Trail in a small pocket called Spring Valley.

The Heitz family bought the Spring Valley property in 1964, having outgrown the original winery in 3 years. When the Heitzes acquired the second ranch it had not changed a great deal since 1898, when a man named

ORIGINAL INGLENOOK cellar has changed little since 1888, though it now hides behind new building.

Anton Rossi finished building a stone cellar as the capstone of his development of the place. Happily for the new owners, capable caretakers had occupied the buildings between 1914, when Rossi quit making wine, and the 1964 purchase. Very little wine was produced on the premises in the interim years.

Except for replanting abandoned vineyards and re-equipping the cellar with stainless steel fermentors and a veritable library of oak casks and barrels, the new owners did not change the appearance of the place they bought until 1972, when progress dictated more space for the making and aging of wine.

There are several ways to go about expanding a winery. An old building can be enlarged or torn down for replacement or abandoned for a new site. The Heitzes elected to keep the fine old stone cellar intact and erect a whole new structure near it. The new building is an octagon of textured block, scheduled in all due time to be the cellar for red wine, while the original holds whites.

The whole property wears an air of secluded well-being. Spring Valley is, in the first place, the sort of place where birds come to sing on a spring morning. Neither the old nor the new cellar disturbs that timeless tranquility. The century-old, white two-story house does so even less.

The replanted vineyard, stretching away south to the end of the little valley, is devoted almost entirely to Grignolino, the cuttings for which came from the vineyard adjoining the original winery, which did prior service as the late Leon Brendel's "only one." It was from the older vines that old Leon made his "only one" Grignolino and Grignolino Rosé, both of which continue as specialties.

Other Heitz varietal table wines come from selected vineyards throughout the Napa Valley. The roster includes Cabernet Sauvignon, Pinot Noir, and Zinfandel among reds, and Johannisberg Riesling and Pinot Chardonnay among whites. Sparkling wines, Sherry, Angelica, and Port round out the list. Most Heitz wines are vintage dated. Some carry the names of individual vineyards. Others have special lot numbers. These and other details are explained in a newsletter.

Regular tasting goes on only at the original winery on St. Helena Highway South, where all of the wines also are available for retail sale. Because the Spring Valley winery buildings are behind the family home, visitors there must acquire an invitation beforehand. Invitations are offered sometimes singly, sometimes in bunches for sun-blessed tastings on the lawns.

Inglenook has grown a great deal in recent years. The most visible evidence is a huge new aging cellar set in front of the old Inglenook structure. From outside, the new building has the dimensions of a dirigible hangar. From within, there is something close to a cathedral quality in its towering racks full of small oak barrels and its vast open spaces.

The winery has seen other changes in keeping up with the times. Some were effected while John Daniel, Jr. continued the ownership of the founding family. Others came after United Vintners bought the place from him in 1954. The latest and largest came after Heublein, Inc. bought United Vintners, and Inglenook with it, in 1969.

Through it all, the original stone-walled building has continued to look pretty much the way romanticists think wineries should look. The front wall has a long row of arched doors and another of arched windows. Several cupolas and other frills serve as relief from the ordinariness of mere roof. Boston ivy, which turns flame red in the fall, covers the blank spots.

Inside, six parallel tunnels contain row upon row of 1,000-gallon oak oval casks. Most of the casks came from the Spesart Mountains in Germany in the last decades of the 19th century and show very nearly flawless craftsmanship. Ordinary cask heads begin to buckle after a certain time; these still follow the curves formed by their German coopers. The wood has blackened with age but not bowed.

The tunnel floors have been loose cinders from Inglenook's founding in 1879, and thereby hangs a tale of changing times. The founder, Captain Gustave Niebaum, a Finnish sea captain and fur trader, was a tidy man. Like all captains he conducted white glove inspections and prided himself on uncommonly clean premises. More recently, government officials have wanted Inglenook to replace the picturesque cinders with concrete, which can be scrubbed clean in the modernized sense of that word.

In Niebaum's day all winemaking was done under the one roof. Now, crushing and fermenting are done several miles away in another United Vintners winery, and only the aging cellars remain on the Rutherford property for visitors to see. (A new crusher and fermenting winery is scheduled for construction across the entry road from the big new building; when completed, it will bring all activities back onto the original property.)

The Inglenook label covers three separate lines of wine. The Napa Valley varietals are presented under the main label. A secondary line of North Coast varietal and generic table wines appears under the Inglenook Vintage label. The Inglenook Navalle wines come mainly from San Joaquin Valley sources.

The tasting room offers a broad sampling of selected wines each day. It is inside the main door of the original building. Tours also start here.

Hanns Kornell Champagne Cellars on Larkmead Lane at the north end of the Napa Valley is devoted almost entirely to sparkling wines.

The old two-story, tree-shaded building started as Larkmead winery early in Napa's vinous history. Other buildings in the complex were added by interim owners, including United Vintners. Hanns Kornell bought the property in 1958. With only a tiny head start from 6 years in a leased winery in Sonoma, Kornell in the next decade built an inventory of a million and a half bottles of aging Champagne. Since 1968, he has augmented that total only slightly.

His is a remarkable one-man achievement. Kornell fled

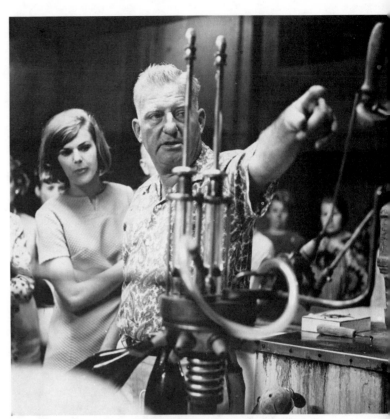

IT'S CHAMPAGNE after the dosage. Hanns Kornell explains the process to visitors at his winery.

OLD COACH HOUSE is backdrop to August Moon Concerts as well as aging cellar at Charles Krug Winery.

THE TASTING GAME

The names of wines do little to explain how they will taste. Gewürztraminer and Sauvignon Blanc do not sound much alike. Sauvignon Blanc and Cabernet Sauvignon sound more alike. But when you get it down to cases, the wines of the first pair taste more like each other than the wines of the latter pair.

Most wineries run tasting rooms to help overcome the semantics of the business. The hosts will help organize a sequence of wines so each sample will show off to its best advantage. (Dry whites first, followed by rosés, reds, sweet wines, appetizers, then desserts. Sparkling wines come last.)

Newcomers usually find it useful to explore at least one candidate from each of the five classes (see the chart on page 59). Experienced tasters sometimes organize a day in the wine country just to taste one class or even one variety.

All "tasting" amounts to is making a considered judgment about whether or not a wine pleases the drinker. This is a purely personal exercise that is most rewarding if it includes some basic tests by which professionals make their decisions.

Sight. The appearance of a wine reveals something of its character. The liquid should be clear to brilliantly clear. Table wines should not have brownish tints (whites range from pale gold to straw yellow, reds from crimson to ruby or slightly purplish, rosés from pink orange to pink). Most dessert wines will have a brownish tint or even be deep amber, depending on type.

Smell. Table wines should have a fresh, fruity quality of aroma. The many types add a wide range of subtle variations. The fruitiness may be overlaid with bouquet. (Aroma is the smell of grapes, bouquet the smell of fermentation and aging.) But one seldom encounters bouquet when drinking new wines at the winery. Appetizer and dessert wines have little aroma, substantial bouquet.

Taste. In fact, taste is simply sweet, sour, bitter, and salty. Most "taste" is an extension of smell. Some qualities can be perceived only after the wine is on the taster's palate: acidity (liveliness versus flatness), astringency (young red wines will have a tannic puckeriness in most types except mellow ones), and weight or body (light versus rich).

One further note. "Dry" describes the absence of sugar, nothing else. Dry wines are sometimes thought to be sour because acidity and tannin are more evident.

OLD PRO coaches student tasters at Martini.

Germany in 1939 and followed a path set by earlier German liberals and political exiles (including winemaker Charles Krug several decades before). Kornell landed in New York broke, worked his way west, in time got work as a maker of sparkling wine, and finally made a start of his own producing Champagne in 1952.

The Larkmead property provides a textbook picture of Champagne making. A guide (sometimes the owner himself, sometimes one of his children) starts visitors out with the new cuvee wine and goes step by step from there. The visitor can peer at the yeast deposit in a still-fermenting bottle, jostle wine in riddling racks, and in general stay within arm's reach of the evolution of a traditional, bottle-fermented sparkling wine. (Photographers might be pleased to know that stone walls frequently provide the backdrop and that the light level is high in areas of active work. They also should know that the light is fluorescent and plays hob with color films.)

There is a tasting room in the small frame office building to the rear of the winery. Visitors can always taste the Kornell still wines and often can investigate one or two of the sparkling ones (Champagne Brut, Sec, or Extra Dry; Pink Champagne; Sparkling Burgundy. The specialty of the house, Sehr Trocken, is opened less often.)

Charles Krug, in a shady grove of tall oaks, presents a classic picture of an old Napa estate winery.

Charles Krug, the man, founded his winery in 1861. He built one massive stone building to keep his wines and another to keep his horses — both at a temperature of 59°.

Krug died in 1892, leaving two daughters to carry on. They continued, with help from a cousin, until Prohibition, when the winery closed. It remained in the hands of a caretaker-owner until Cesare Mondavi bought the property in 1943. Since his death in 1959, his wife, Rosa, and their children have held the reins.

Various aspects of the Krug ranch have changed over the years, but the two stone buildings remain and are the core of the present winery. The old winery building continues in its original role. The one-time coach house at present holds small cooperage for aging select wines. In addition, the Mondavis have erected a pair of large buildings to hold more oak barrels and the bottling part of the operation. Small frame buildings house the winemaker's lab, the offices, and, most important to visitors, the tasting room. The surrounding grounds are handsomely landscaped.

The lawns and gardens serve a variety of uses. Favorite customers and friends are invited to a series of tastings on the lawn on summer Sundays. The August Moon Concerts combine first-rate chamber music with wine tasting on successive Saturday evenings during August. Finally, the big picnic and barbecue ground alongside the old coach house accommodates many groups that have reserved and patiently awaited their turn.

No matter how busy the lawns, Krug never requires reservations for its ably led and unusually complete winery tour. During the harvest the fermentors are out of bounds. Otherwise, visitors get to see every department, in which a fine balance exists between old and new. The red wine fermentors, for example, are upright, open-topped redwood tanks. Very few are left in California. They contrast with long rows of glass-lined steel tanks in which Krug wines wait from the time they have had enough wood aging until their turn comes up on the bottling schedule.

The redwood fermentors are scheduled to disappear one day in favor of stainless steel. Meantime, they are a picturesque reminder of what once was the norm.

The tasting room offers a selection of three or four wines on any one day; they come from a complete range of varietal table wines. The list includes Chenin Blanc, Gewürztraminer, Chardonnay, Johannisberg Riesling, Zinfandel, Cabernet Sauvignon, and Pinot Noir. Several are vintage dated. There are among the reds some special selections (not opened for tasting) with extra age. Krug also has generic table wines and Sherries and Port under the main label. The Mondavis also offer table wines under their secondary label, CK.

Louis M. Martini dates only from 1934 as a winery and yet is honored as one of the old-school labels in the Napa Valley. Family continuity is the key.

The founder, the late Louis M. Martini, began his career as a California winemaker in 1906 in Guasti and owned his first winery as early as 1922. Those facts, along with his immediate post-Prohibition start in the Napa Valley, earned him a secure reign as dean of Cali-

LOUIS M. MARTINI cellars hold a fascinating array of old casks, tanks, and bins full of aging wines.

fornia winemakers. His son and successor, Louis P., continues the family ownership in the traditional vein and in the original cellars.

Hosts at Martini do not insist on touring visitors through the buildings. They often skip that whole segment of the proceedings. Persuade them, if necessary, for the Martini cellars are instructive in several ways. The original Louis built his winery without costly adornments, but he built it to last. As a result, much of the early-day equipment lingers as accompaniment to newer kinds.

Most of the Martini fermentors, for example, are now of stainless steel. Yet, for a couple of years at least, the original open concrete fermentors for reds will be around and in use. (The proprietor recalls how well they were constructed, and he shudders at the prospect of de-

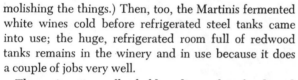

FRANCISCAN'S *modern winery was built in 1973.*

PHELPS *makes handsome use of rustic wood design.*

molishing the things.) Then, too, the Martinis fermented white wines cold before refrigerated steel tanks came into use; the huge, refrigerated room full of redwood tanks remains in the winery and in use because it does a couple of jobs very well.

The main aging cellar holds a diverse lot of redwood and oak cooperage, as well as the bottling line, to round out a complete look at all phases of winemaking. (The tour does not go to a pair of flanking buildings that contain the majority of Martini small oak cooperage, nor does it go down into a cellar that runs most of the main building's length beneath the central part of the main floor. In this latter room are the oak casks and bins of bottles full of specially aged Martini Private Reserve and particularly prized Special Selection wines, purchased more easily at the winery than elsewhere.)

In the tasting room, a new-in-1973 structure adjoining the main cellar, the complete roster of Martini wines is available for appraisal. The roster includes vintage-dated Folle Blanche, Gewürztraminer, Johannisberg Riesling, and a dry Chenin Blanc in whites, and Barbera, Cabernet Sauvignon, Pinot Noir, and Zinfandel in reds. The supporting cast includes generic table wines, Sherries, and Ports.

Folle blanche, incidentally, is the grape used in Cognacs in France and is made into a varietal table wine only by this winery in California.

Mayacamas Vineyards clings to the topmost ridges of the Mayacamas Mountains. Just getting to the winery taxes the suspension systems of most automobiles of ordinary manufacture. The road from the winery up to the highest vineyards is even more adventurous.

One visitor, awestruck by the tumultuous terrain, said that working there was "a hard way to serve the Lord." The owners and staff agree but enjoy it.

The owners are Bob and Nonie Travers, who acquired the site in 1968 from another family ownership.

The property centers upon an old stone winery erected by a man named J. M. Fisher in 1889 and operated as Mt. Veeder vineyards until 1910 or so. Restoration proceedings began in 1941 when a couple named Jack and Mary Taylor bought the property and named it Mayacamas. They got the central building back in condition in 1947 and ran the estate until the Traverses bought it.

Mayacamas is cupped in the rocky rib of a long-extinct volcano, Mt. Veeder, and surrounded by several blocks of vineyard, mostly Cabernet Sauvignon. In a couple of places, sheer rock walls stick up out of the earth to set firm limits on vineyard size. Several hundred feet higher than the winery, ridge-top terraces carry the Chardonnay vineyards.

The owners will run guided tours of the winery by appointment. In addition to being a good example of

ROBERT MONDAVI visitors cross courtyard to tasting room at end of tour through ultramodern cellars.

traditional stonework, it provides a clear example of how a small winery might be arranged. The modern crusher and press are in a small building on the uphill side of the main structure. The primary cellar is full of a diverse mixture of cooperage ranging from 1,500 gallons capacity down to 60-gallon oak.

The primary wines of Mayacamas are Chardonnay and Cabernet Sauvignon, both vintage dated. Now and again, when the weather is right, Mayacamas makes a late-harvest Zinfandel.

Robert Mondavi Winery in Oakville crushed its first wine in 1966 while the carpenters still were struggling to get the roof on the building.

It does not look that new, mainly because founder Robert Mondavi commissioned designer Cliff May to pay architectural tribute to the role Franciscan missions had in developing California as a wine district.

On the other hand, most of the building is newer than 1966. Steady growth has required Mondavi to build an unending series of new structures.

A faintly churchlike tower serves as the anchor point for two wings, one straight and one bent.

The south wing houses the tasting and sales rooms, as well as other rooms designed for use in celebrations of large and small events. The sales room is furnished with early California pieces of interest. Also, one wall has a demonstration for serious wine collectors. It is a stacked

mass of agricultural tiles — light proof, excellent insulators, and sized exactly to hold wine bottles. Further, the design is imposing.

To the north, the bent wing holds the offices and then a whole series of fermenting and aging cellars. Robert Mondavi, the man, is a ceaseless experimenter. As a result, his winery is an ever-changing one, full of wizard equipment for visitors to gaze upon and learn from. Up in the roof rafters of the fermenting room, for example, are several horizontal tanks powered so they can be rotated. These, having failed to give good enough quality, have fallen into disuse. French continuous presses and German centrifuges, having helped make good wine, are active parts of the operating winery. The guides at Mondavi ably explain all of the hows and whys of the place.

A spacious open arch separates the two wings, framing a view across long rows of vines to the steep flanks of the Mayacamas Mountains beyond. A plush lawn between the wings is the site of summer concerts, art shows, and frequent special tastings.

The wine list at Mondavi includes Chenin Blanc, Johannisberg Riesling, Chardonnay, and Fumé Blanc; a Gamay Rosé; and the reds Cabernet Sauvignon, Pinot Noir, and Zinfandel. All are vintage dated. There are no generics, nor are there appetizer or dessert wines.

A word of explanation: Fumé Blanc is a dry edition

CAVES BORE into hill behind trim, white Schramsberg fermenting winery. Champagne caves are nearby.

AT NICHELINI winery, the last working Roman press in California dwarfs a weekend visitor.

of Sauvignon Blanc. The wine labeled here as Sauvignon Blanc is sweet and intended to be served after dinner.

Nichelini Vineyard is way up in the east hills. East of Conn Dam and the reservoir, State 128 runs along bare shoulders of hills forming one side of a large canyon. Just at the head of the canyon, the road slips into a grove of oaks. There amid the trees and set into the downslope is Nichelini.

Steps descend the slope between an age-enfeebled barn and a solid frame house. The wine aspects of the place do not reveal themselves forcibly until the foot of the stairs, where it turns out that within the rock foundations of the house, a substantial cellar is full of redwood and oak cooperage.

Tasting goes on, under clear skies or cloudy, on a terrace just outside the cellar door and within the immense framework of one of the last Roman presses in this hemisphere. It worked until the early 1950s. Though it still could be used, the Nichelinis would rather have it serve only ornamental purposes. (There is scarcely a slower, more laborious way to press grapes.)

Nichelini, founded in the late 19th century and now in the hands of the third generation, makes a number of varietal table wines. Sauvignon Vert is the specialty in the whites; Cabernet Sauvignon, Zinfandel, and Gamay

are among the reds.

There are no formal tours, but poking around is encouraged. The family winery is open weekends and holidays only, when 12 visitors at a time can make use of a tree-shaded picnic table as one of the rewards for driving all the way up there.

Joseph Phelps Winery, set against a vine-covered slope in the first row of hills on the east side of the Napa Valley, was built in 1974. Its contractor-proprietor came to wine as a builder of other wineries and was so attracted by it that he stayed to build his own cellar.

The wood building is in effect two pavilions joined by a closed bridge that holds offices and labs. On the uphill side, a reconstructed trestle from another construction site has been turned into a Brobdingnagian arbor (due, in time, to be covered by wisteria).

One pavilion holds the fermentors — steel ones in an otherwise woody environment — along with a few small tanks of upright oak and even fewer oak oval casks from Germany.

The other pavilion holds lofty racks full of oak barrels. The bottling room is alongside.

For the most part, the walls are of large-dimensioned, rough-sawn redwood. But in the offices and reception rooms, walls and ceilings are of fine paneling with richly detailed decorative trims.

GONDOLAS holding 1 to 5 tons of grapes now deliver nearly all Napa Valley grapes from vines to wineries.

STAG'S LEAP wine cellar entryway near the Silverado Trail is shaded by an oak grove.

Tours are by appointment. There is no regular tasting of the short list of varietal wines.

Pope Valley Winery is located in the valley of the same name parallel to and east of the Napa Valley. It is a peaceful place with rolling hills dotted with oak, madrone, and digger pine trees, here and there patches of wild grapevines, and very little else.

The weathered, old-fashioned wood barn exterior of the three-story winery fits comfortably into its hillside setting, as it has since 1909. From then until 1959 it was operated as the Sam Haus Winery by Sam himself and his sister.

In 1972 James and Arlene Devitt and their two sons bought the property and reequipped and restored the workings of the winery to modern standards. But slowly. Devitt comes to winemaking from the electronics business, and the latter has helped to support the former in the transition years.

Small lots of Chenin Blanc, Sauvignon Vert, Semillon, Gamay, Cabernet Sauvignon, Zinfandel, and Zinfandel Rosé are made principally from Napa Valley grapes. Most are vintage dated.

It is a longish drive over a winding two-lane mountain road from the Napa Valley, so visitors, especially on weekdays, should phone ahead to be sure the gate is open.

V. Sattui Winery just south of St. Helena opened in 1976 and was quickly discovered by wine country visitors.

In addition to the winery and tasting room, the attractive building houses a gift, cheese, and deli shop. Flanking the white stucco, mission-style structure are many large, tree-shaded picnic tables for use by winery and cheese shop customers.

The label dates not from 1976 but 1885 when Vittorio Sattui established it for his own wines. It, as others, disappeared during Prohibition, but has been revived in a new building by Vittorio's great grandson Daryl and a limited partnership.

The initial offering of Sattui wines was purchased from other Napa Valley sources, but the Sattui label will go onto varietals, particularly Zinfandel and Cabernet made on the premises. The first of these were crushed in 1975. They gain age in oak barrels in full view of the visitor tasting area that occupies a corner of the winery proper. The owner often does the pouring while he explains the winery operation.

Schramsberg Vineyards, having been founded by Jacob Schram in 1862, won quick immortality in the writings of Robert Louis Stevenson after the great British novelist's visit to the winery in 1880.

For a long time the immortality was more literary

VISITORS to V. Sattui Winery, south of St. Helena, can relax and lunch at tree-shaded picnic tables.

than practical. Stevenson's *The Silverado Squatters* has gone on and on, but the winery began to fade as soon as Schram died. It closed altogether in 1921, experienced two ephemeral revivals in 1940 and 1951, and then closed again.

Jack Davies launched Schramsberg anew in August, 1965, this time as a sparkling wine cellar. (Schram had made only still wines.) The old property has lived up to Stevenson's notions since then.

It's a romantic place to visit. Stevenson's original description of the trail up from the main road remains fairly accurate, though the surface is a good deal better. The oaks, sycamores, other trees, and undergrowth are a fair demonstration of the local plant ecology. The little stone barn that was Captain McEachran's winery stands firm, just left of the road and just downhill from the Schram homestead.

The original winery building still stands at the top of a large clearing next to the old Schram home. Two tunnels going back into the hill from the winery have been turned into modern fermenting rooms for production of the wines that become Champagne a few hundred yards away.

A short lane leads to the Champagne cellar itself. The wood-faced building encloses a set of three more tunnels that hold the aging Champagne in bottles, thousands of them piled row on row in the *methode champenoise* fashion.

Supplies of Schramsberg Champagnes are limited. The four styles include Blanc de Blancs from white grapes, Blanc de Noir from Pinot noir grapes, Cuvee de Gamay — dry wines all — and a dessert cremant Champagne finished Demi-Sec.

Much of the early hillside vineyard well up the ridge from the winery has been replanted, principally to Chardonnay and Pinot noir.

Davies conducts tours of the winery past and present when he has a spare moment. An appointment is required. Supplies are too limited to permit tasting. Sometimes there is not enough to permit sales.

Spring Mountain Vineyards, after several peripatetic years, moved in 1975 into its permanent home, the old Tiburcio Parrott estate on Spring Mountain.

Parrott, an enthusiastic participant in whatever made the late 19th century a Golden Age of Most Things, built a magnificent house at one edge of a meadow and a fine barn and cellar at the other edge. The house has been kept in good repair through all the years since. The long-idle barn and cellars required considerable restoration when Spring Mountain proprietor Michael Robbins and his family took possession. The work is underway but not likely to be completed before the end of the decade.

Meantime, visitors are welcome to check on progress after they have made an appointment. There is no tasting, but the wines made on leased properties and aged in a tiny cellar beneath the Robbinses' earlier residence are available for retail purchase. The list includes Chardonnay, Sauvignon Blanc, and Cabernet Sauvignon.

Stag's Leap Wine Cellars sits neatly in its hillside location among a grove of oaks. The 1976 addition of a barrel-aging cellar to the original building makes the winery more visible to passing traffic.

The main building contains two rows of upright oak tanks, a row of fine old oak oval casks, and several racks of barrels. Outside, on the uphill side, two rows of stainless steel fermentors run the length of the building.

Stag's Leap is so thoughtfully designed that it offers a virtual textbook example of how to put together a small, specialized winery. One example: both crusher and press straddle a single channel cut into the concrete work pad. Stems, pomace, and wash water all course downhill, out of the way until the work is done and they can be disposed of at leisure.

Production at Stag's Leap is not great enough to permit tasting, but proprietor Warren Winiarski will explain to all who call ahead how the winery works and how he makes his short list of wines: Johannisberg Riesling, Cabernet Sauvignon, Gamay Beaujolais, and Merlot.

As the proprietor finds vineyard sources, he plans to add other varietals to this list.

There is, it should be noted, another Stag's Leap, called Stags' Leap Vineyard. It is the property of the Peter Doumani family and does not yet have its permanent cellars in operation.

Sterling Vineyards, atop a lofty hill just south of Calistoga, looks from the outside like a fair approximation of the sort of churches Crusaders left on the Greek Isles.

Inside, the three partners have assembled a collection of the most modern winemaking equipment, save for the aging cellars, where the time-honored barrel dominates.

The whole establishment is set up to make wine first and foremost, but it also is set up to provide an on-going show for visitors. The showmanship begins at the beginning. Visitors get from the car park up to the winery on an aerial tramway. The tour, then, is self-operated. A long, elevated walkway threads its way through the entire premises, with visual displays at every stop to explain what takes place within view. The attention to visual detail goes so far as to include colored glass windows in each of the barrel aging cellars, making for a tranquil kind of light show.

The bells of St. Dunstans — the audible extra — episodically ring to entertain whoever is on hand at the moment.

So it goes.

Still, the essential function of the place is winemaking. As much or more attention has been lavished on the design of the working elements. To cite one example, the winery runs downhill from the crushers and stainless

STERLING VINEYARDS *main cellar, patterned after Greek architecture, is reached by a tramway.*

GRAPE LUGS are seldom seen at larger wineries now but continue in use at many of the smaller cellars.

FERMENTING CHARDONNAY at Stony Hill dispels CO_2 through "bubbler" bottles atop oak casks.

steel fermentors to the last of the small barrel aging cellars. The announced purpose is to allow gravity rather than pumps to move the wine as much as possible.

In a separate building atop an even higher knoll than the winery's, the tasting room is an elegantly airy place with awesome views down the valley. In it, the proprietors offer for tasting selected wines from a list that includes Chardonnay, Chenin Blanc, Gewürztraminer, Sauvignon Blanc, Cabernet Sauvignon, Merlot, Pinot Noir, and Zinfandel. The $2.50 charge to ride the tram can be applied against purchase of a bottle of wine.

Stonegate Winery, new in 1973, squeezes itself into a one-time tractor shed on Dunaweal Lane, just a few yards from the lane's intersection with State 29.

The proprietors have left the exterior of the place unornamented but have turned the interior into an attractive, neatly organized, small winery. Six oak tanks fill one room. Approximately 200 close-stacked barrels, most of them from Europe, make an even tighter fit in the second room. A battery of stainless steel fermentors sits outside; the office and sales room is at the opposite end of the building from the steel tanks.

Though the winery is too small to provide tasting, an affable staff — which is to say one of the owning Spaulding family — will stop to talk shop whenever the work is not too pressing. The list of wines on hand for sale includes Chenin Blanc, Sauvignon Blanc, Cabernet Sauvignon, and Pinot Noir.

Stony Hill Vineyards cannot be fitted easily into a day of casual touring. Owner Frederick McCrea has his winery on the family homesite, which he acquired as a peaceable place to spend his retirement. To keep a modicum of peace, he asks that potential visitors write ahead for an appointment to see Stony Hill.

The winery, housed at the foot of a vineyard of Johannisberg Riesling, went up in 1951. It is a small block building with an efficient crusher-press alongside the back wall and a handsome pair of carved doors in the front side. One room holds the aging cooperage (all small oak casks and barrels); the other holds binned wines and often a barrel or two.

McCrea now makes three vintage-dated wines, all white. They are Chardonnay, Gewürztraminer, and White Riesling. He ferments them in small oak barrels, dispelling the CO_2 through bubbler hoses with their noses stuck into water-filled wine bottles, and finally ages his wines in similar wood. Once a year he dispatches a letter to a small mailing list and sells the annual ration of Stony Hill in a few weeks.

Thus there is no tasting. The tour, even including the swimming pool, takes only a few minutes. (It takes twice as long to drive up the winding private road to the house, 700 feet off the valley floor northwest of St. Helena.)

Sutter Home Winery, straight across State 29 from Louis M. Martini, offers various contrasts to its neighbor.

The winery is housed in a handsomely proportioned board-and-batten structure originally built to house the cellars of J. Thomann, one of the major forces in the early history of Napa wine. The building proves beyond doubt the durability of good wood properly assembled.

Sutter Home belongs, these days, to the Trinchero family. Theirs since 1945, it comes by its name honestly. John Sutter and son Albert built their first winery in the east hills of the valley in 1890. Sutter's son-in-law transferred the winery — lock, stock, and barrels — to its present site in 1906-07 and operated it until 1930.

The Trincheros operate their historic winery, with its historic name, as a small and highly specialized affair. Nearly all of the production is Zinfandel. The exception is a small annual lot of Moscato Canelli. This specialization is a relatively recent development. They formerly offered a full range of wines.

The two specialties, along with a handful of residual stocks from earlier times, are on hand to be tasted daily. There is no tour of the immaculately kept cellars.

Villa Mt. Eden began as a vineyard in 1881 and endured as that and a winery through numerous ownerships. It is now the property of James and Anne McWilliams, who bought it in 1970.

They installed sophisticated new equipment for a winery comeback in 1974. Grapes are crushed into rolling stainless steel tanks in the vineyards, then fermented in other steel tanks before aging in traditional oak barrels.

The one-story, white stucco winery is one of several buildings surrounding an open courtyard. Vineyards adjoin the winery.

Current wine production is small and plans are to keep it that way. All wines are varietals and focus on Chenin Blanc, Chardonnay, Gewürztraminer, Napa Gamay, and Cabernet Sauvignon. The winemaker-vineyard manager is Nils Venge.

The small staff can handle visitors by appointment on weekdays only.

Miscellaneous Wineries. The late 1960s and early 1970s were an extraordinary boom time for wine in California and especially in the Napa Valley. The valley is full of young vineyards and new wineries. Many of the wineries formed during the boom have settled down enough to welcome visitors, but several still are in their formative states or else too small to accommodate the public.

Trefethen Vineyard lies between Napa City and Yountville; Domaine Chandon, Cakebread Cellars, and Charles Woods' Napa Wine Cellars all cluster around Yountville; Caymus Vineyards is near Rutherford; Mt. Veeder is in the Mayacamas Mountains; Veedercrest has vines in the Mayacamas Mountains and a cellar in Berkeley; Conn Creek, Raymond Vineyard, and Yverdon are near St. Helena; and finally Diamond Creek is at Calistoga.

In addition to these, several bulk wineries appear to the wondering eye of visitors. United Vintners owns two,

SUTTER HOME winery buildings were built by Napa Valley pioneer winemaker J. Thomann in 1880s.

one adjoining Oakville, the other at Deer Park Road north of St. Helena. The Napa Valley Cooperative is on the highway south of St. Helena. Last, the old Sunny St. Helena winery south of St. Helena town now serves only as a storage cellar for another company.

Other Than Wineries

The happy town of St. Helena is the hub of the Napa Valley, but attractions for visitors range from Yountville north beyond Calistoga.

A citizen's action committee called the Napa Valley Wine Library Association some years ago founded a specialized wine library. Much of the collection came from the bookshelves of local winemakers. The rest was (and continues to be) purchased with membership fees.

The St. Helena Public Library, where the collection is housed, is open to all from 10 A.M. to 9 P.M. Monday through Thursday and from 10 A.M. to 5:30 P.M. Friday. Saturday hours are 10 A.M. to 4 P.M.

A side benefit to dues payers is admission to a highly convivial annual wine tasting.

Members also get first crack at the special Wine Appreciation Courses held each year. The courses start Friday afternoon and run through Sunday several weekends a year, mostly in June and August. The faculty is drawn from winery staffs, and the level of information is very high indeed.

For details about joining the association ($5 per head), the Napa Valley Wine Library Association, P.O. Box 328, St. Helena, CA 94574.

CLASSMATES TALK over the effects of food on taste of wine at Napa Valley Wine Library study course.

TUNNEL OF ELMS at north side of St. Helena is a scenic part of the Napa Valley tour.

Another literary possibility offers itself nearby. The Silverado Museum, a practical monument to Robert Louis Stevenson, occupies part of a fine stone building called the Hatchery, located on Railroad Avenue a block east of Main Street in St. Helena.

The museum full of Stevenson materials and memorabilia is located in the Napa Valley partly because founder Norman Strouse likes the region but primarily because Stevenson lived and worked here in 1880-81. The collection has been praised widely as the finest private one in the world. A volunteer staff helps researchers and visitors daily (except Mondays and holidays) from noon to 4 P.M.

Robert Louis Stevenson State Park, on the flanks of Mt. St. Helena, is where Stevenson and his bride stayed while he wrote *The Silverado Squatters*. The park is undeveloped. In fact, it is less developed than it was before major forest fires roared through the area in 1964. The park is mainly interesting for Stevenson's having stayed there, for the old mines he describes in his book, and for evidences of the way local ecology restores itself when man wanders away for awhile.

The approach is north of Calistoga, from the highway to Lake County.

Bothe-Napa Valley State Park is the biggest and most varied of several parks in the county. The gates are 4 miles north of St. Helena on State 29. The park proper ranges well back into the west hills. Picnic and camping facilities, hiking trails, and a swimming pool are its prime attractions, good enough to make it one of the most heavily used parks in the state system.

An adjunct, a few hundred yards to the south, is the Old Bale Mill. Built by pioneer Dr. Edward Bale, the mill with its towering overshot waterwheel has been rebuilt from a stage of advanced decay so that it looks workable. Although no new grain has found its way between the grinding stones since the founding era, the mill does contain a considerable number of mementoes of 19th century Napa.

Conn Dam Recreation Area, up off the valley floor in the east hills, has cooling water and some picnic tables. The turnoff from the Silverado Trail is marked State 128-Conn Dam.

The Napa Valley Olive Oil Manufactory is not technically a fair, but it has many of the same charms as one. From a white frame building, the owning Italian family sells not only its own fragrant olive oil but also an international mélange of cheeses, pastes, dried mushrooms, breadsticks, and other delectables.

The Olive Oil Manufactory is at the end of Charter Oak Avenue in the southeast corner of the main business district of St. Helena.

On the north side of St. Helena, the Hurd Candle Factory and an allied gourmet shop occupy the top floor of the stone building that contains the Freemark Abbey winery. The Hurds' staff molds beeswax into some highly improbable shapes.

The valley has several art galleries specializing wholly or substantially in local scenes. One is located in Vintage 1870 along with a flurry of crafts and antique shops, clothiers, and other specialty merchants. That Vintage 1870 once was a winery is celebrated by the G. Groezinger Wine Co., a retail shop named after the founder of these buildings. Vintage 1870 is on the main street of Yountville, alongside State 29.

The Napa Valley Cheese Co. north of Yountville sells an international collection of cheeses, with lunches to travel or not.

On another level altogether, the Napa Valley's hills offer the right kind of air to glider pilots. The little airport at Calistoga is headquarters for a sizable contingent of silent fliers, whose takeoffs and landings are the best show in the valley for winery-weary small fry.

Plotting a Route

Napa County sandwiches neatly between U.S. 101 to the west and Interstate 80 to the east. State Highways 12, 29, 121, and 128 connect it variously with the major highways.

Of the possible combinations of access routes, Interstate 80, then State 29 from Vallejo to Napa is the most direct, the flattest, and the least scenic. It works for anyone starting from Sacramento or San Francisco and Oakland. Another route from San Francisco that is slower, hillier, and prettier goes across the Golden Gate, then north on U.S. 101, State 37, and State 121. From the north, U.S. 101 and State 128 combine easily and picturesquely.

The Napa Valley, being long and narrow, has two major roads of its own. They parallel each other on a north-south axis.

State 29, the westerly one, has almost all the wineries on it. It cuts a straight swath a few hundred yards from the feet of the westerly hills. Its border is mostly vineyards, partly towns.

The eastern parallel route is the Silverado Trail, which loops along a leisurely and almost purely uncommercial way. It runs right at the foot of the east hills, elevated just enough to give fine vineyard panoramas.

This was the old stagecoach road Robert Louis Stevenson described in *The Silverado Squatters*. In spots it provides reminders of its earlier service, but for the most part it has now been widened and straightened to suit the modern automobile.

Several crossroads tie the two together, making it easy to swap back and forth.

Still other roads poke up into the hills on either side of the valley. Nearly all offer pleasant panoramas, though very few go anywhere specific. The Oakville-Trinity Road goes to Sonoma. In due time the Spring Mountain Road gets into the vicinity of Santa Rosa.

From the east side of the valley, State 128 provides a slow, bucolic route to Davis or other Central Valley points.

OLD BALE MILL, now a state park, used towering overshot wheel to grind grain for Napa pioneers.

VINTAGE 1870, a one-time winery, was handsomely revived to house shops, eateries, and a theater.

EAST BAY

Mostly urban, but still famous for gravelly soil and white wines

Alameda and Contra Costa are predominantly urban counties, full of such downtown places as Oakland and Richmond. And yet both counties are old and durable sources of wine in the places where urbanization has left open spaces.

No one of their wineries exists in a completely countrified setting, but all of them have some rural charms to go with the urban ones.

There is one distinct wine district, the Livermore Valley. Otherwise, wineries string out along the bay-facing hills from Warm Springs on the south edge of Alameda County all the way to Martinez, on the Carquinez Strait, toward the mouth of the Sacramento River.

In the town of Livermore, you'll find a pair of wineries; in nearby Pleasanton, a third. Local roads allow the easy incorporation of a fourth cellar in Warm Springs into a day of touring.

To the north of this region is Martinez with two wineries in its hinterlands. These can be coupled with two in Solano County, across the Sacramento River, to make a tidy loop drive. (For this reason Solano County has been severed from its traditional companion, Napa, and incorporated into this chapter.)

 ### LIVERMORE AND PLEASANTON

Livermore is a small town of surprising contrasts. It is the site of a durable rodeo, which has genuine cowboys as participants and San Francisco commuters as much

of its audience. The town is the home site of two nuclear research stations. Finally, in the happiest of its roles, it is one of the earliest of the state's wine-producing towns.

Say "Livermore" to a student of California wine, and he will make the automatic associations of "white wine" and "gravelly soil."

Pioneer vineyardists Charles Wetmore and Louis Mel brought cuttings of vines from Chateau d'Yquem very early in Livermore's wine history and made Sauterne-like wines from the resulting grapes. The original Carl H. Wente and the original James Concannon concentrated on white wines, too. In the intervening years, the winemakers have branched out from white wines but never left them.

The local definition of gravel includes river-rounded stones up to softball size, maybe slightly larger. Such soil is ruinous to discs, harrows, and other tilling equipment, but it runs 650 feet deep. Whatever the effect on tools, the local vineyardists set store by it as an environment for grape roots.

In terms of size, the district has never accounted for much of the state's wine total. The whole county of Alameda produces less than 2 percent of the state's wine each year. The steady growth of population, commuter and local, poses a real threat to that level. However, the families making wine in Livermore now are the families that made wine there in the beginning, in the 1880s. That kind of continuity leads people to pace themselves for a long race. Even nuclear phyzzing in

A PAINTER'S VISION of summer — green vines, gold hills, blue sky — unfolds in the Livermore Valley.

the neighborhood has not dimmed the distant view.

The concession has been the purchase by Wente Bros. of new vineyard acreage in Monterey County.

Pleasanton, 5 miles west of Livermore on the other side of a low ridge, is closely related in both time and temperament. It is home to Villa Armando, a durable if slightly less famed winery than Concannon and Wente Bros.

The Wineries

Livermore's two wineries, pioneer firms still in the hands of their founding families, are Concannon and Wente Bros. They are described first, followed by the Pleasanton winery called Villa Armando.

Concannon Vineyard, in the hands of the third generation with the fourth coming up, proves conclusively that Irishmen can make wine, given a reasonable climate to do it in.

As with any Irish enterprise, there is a fine story about how it got started. In the 1880s the then Archbishop of San Francisco, Joseph S. Alemany, was a bit short of sacramental wine. His solution was to suggest to James Concannon, printer and maker of rubber stamps, that he should buy a vineyard and make wines. Concannon had a flexible enough mind to make the professional jump, and did in 1883. The printer has gone out of all subsequent Concannons while the winemaker has stayed in them. They have stayed in one place, in

the southeast quarter of Livermore, 2 miles south of the city flagpole on Tesla Road.

Their winery appears unhurried and informal. The oldest part of the building dates from the early years of the winery. Subsequent additions have been made out of need for space rather than any desire to add frills. Some sections of wall are brick. Others are clapboard. A fair proportion is of corrugated iron, to match the roof. Within, old oak upright tanks and oval casks from the founder's day run in orderly but crowded rows. So do the stacks of filled case boxes, which share space with a mainly unmechanical bottling and labeling department. A trestle table in the midst of the cased goods serves as the tasting room. (Visitors sometimes find themselves face to face with a Concannon when they come to it.)

In case anyone is deceived by these appearances, it should be noted that the family has its feet in the 20th century. Not only is it abreast of research at U.C. Davis and other centers — it participates. The Concannons have contributed a few acres from their small vineyards to serve as test plots for grape varieties not commonly grown in Livermore and for experimental combinations of rootstocks and fruiting varieties. (Vines, like humans, marry for better or for worse. California, afflicted with both phylloxera and nematodes, needs resistant rootstocks to carry its classic grapes. Some combinations work. Some do not. Some work in some conditions but not in others. Researchers are very busy at the mating game.)

ORDERLY ROWS of upright oak casks line a wall of Concannon winery. Most shown hold dry Sherry.

The winery itself has a modern stainless steel fermenting area at one side to balance the traditional aging cellars.

Most Concannon wines are white — no surprise in Livermore — but the winery offers other sorts. The whites include Chateau Concannon (a sweet wine of semillon grapes), Chenin Blanc, Johannisberg (White) Riesling, and Sauvignon Blanc. The Concannons were first to offer the red Petite Sirah as a varietal in 1964. Other reds are Cabernet Sauvignon and Zinfandel. Finally, there is a Zinfandel Rosé. The Concannons occasionally offer to their mailing list a limited bottling. In recent times, these have included Sauvignon Blancs, Cabernet Sauvignons, and a dessert wine called Muscat de Frontignan.

Wente Bros. has been the neighbor to Concannon for as long as there has been a Concannon in this town. Carl H. Wente, in fact, arrived a year or so ahead of James Concannon.

They were of an age. The subsequent generations of the two families have grown up within a stone's throw of each other. But there is no stone-throwing. The two families get along well enough that it is traditional for the oldest child to take charge of both broods when the parents go somewhere together.

Wente's winery, on the opposite side of Tesla Road from Concannon and a few hundred yards east, retained its original building until 1966. By then the old frame building had become a small part of the winery and had to yield to a more efficient structure. With its dismantling, all of Wente took on a modern appearance. There have been subsequent additions to the tilt-up concrete cellars. The age of the ivy on the walls helps peg the construction dates.

Few wineries offer visitors a clearer picture than Wente does of how wine is made from start to finish. Behind the main aging cellars, new presses adjoin several rows of fermenting tanks. Wente presses grapes in an unusual series of big horizontal steel cylinders designed to exert precisely measurable pressure. The fresh juice flows directly to one of the steel tanks, in which temperature is governed by liquid coolant pumped through a jacket welded to the outer wall. The whole works is out-of-doors and accessible for close inspection.

The Wentes also have some specialized gadgetry in the fermentor area, used to haul fresh juice up from their distant vineyards in the Salinas Valley of Monterey County. Guides on the weekday-only tours gladly explain the workings of it all.

After the aging cellars, which contain redwood, oak, and glass-lined steel for one purpose and another, the visitor can get within arm's reach of an automatic bottling line. Automatic bottling lines have a hypnotic effect on mechanically-minded people. The lines have dozens of moving parts, all going at a synchronized rate. Bottles get washed, filled, corked or capped, topped with a capsule, labeled fore and aft, all with little or no human assistance. Except for the off-switch, it is a scene out of *The Sorcerer's Apprentice.*

Wente's tasting room is an adobe building designed expressly to comfort guests. The basic notion is an Arthurian round table at which all comers are welcome to taste Chardonnay, Grey Riesling, Pinot Blanc, Sauvignon Blanc, Semillon, and the proprietary Le Blanc de Blancs among whites, and Petite Sirah, Pinot Noir, and Zinfandel among reds.

With the maturing of their Monterey County vines, the Wentes have added specially labeled Gewürztraminers and Johannisberg Rieslings.

Villa Armando in Pleasanton is little known among Californians. Most of the wine made at this cellar is sent to the East.

Anthony D. Scotto acquired the winery from its founding family in 1962, coining the current name then. In 1971 Scotto opened a new tasting room, designed in Spanish style, in which his wines first became available to the home audience. It continues to be a prime source.

Tours of the old, workaday winery buildings directly behind the Pleasanton Hotel are by appointment only.

NORTH ALAMEDA

DAVIS BYNUM. S side of Solano Ave. at Ordway in Albany. (1580 Solano Ave., Albany 94706. Tel [415] 526-1366) M-Sa, 10:30-6. Ta

OAK BARREL. University Ave. 1 block E of San Pablo Ave. in Berkeley. (1201 University Ave., Berkeley 94702. Tel [415] 849-0400) M-Sa, 10-7; Su, 11-7. Ta

LIVERMORE-ALAMEDA

CONCANNON. From Livermore flag plaza, S 2 mi. on Livermore Ave.-Tesla Rd. (4590 Tesla Rd., Livermore 94550. Tel [415] 447-3760) Ltd. picnic. M-Sa, 9-4; Su 12-4:30. GT (on the hour)/Ta

STONY RIDGE. From Main St. in Pleasanton, E on Ray St.-Vineyard Ave. 3½ mi. Winery at end of pvt. drive, S off rd. (1188 Vineyard Ave., Pleasanton 94566. Tel [415] 846-2133) Weekdays, 9-4:30; Weekends, 11-5.

VILLA ARMANDO. From Main St. in Pleasanton, N ½ block on St. John St. (behind Pleasanton Hotel). (553 St. John St., Pleasanton 94566. Tel [415] 846-5488) Daily 9-5. Tours by appt./Ta

WEIBEL. From Mission San Jose, S 1 mi. on S.R. 238, E on Stanford Ave. ½ mi. (1250 Stanford Ave., Mission San Jose 94538. Tel [415] 656-9914) Picnic. Daily, 10-4 (tours M-F, 10-3). GT/Ta

WENTE BROS. From Livermore flag plaza, S 2½ mi. on Livermore Ave.-Tesla Rd. (5565 Tesla Rd., Livermore 94550. Tel [415] 447-3603) M-Sa, 9-5; Su, 10-5. GT (M-F)/Ta

KEY: *GT (guided tour); IT (informal tour); Ta (tasting).*

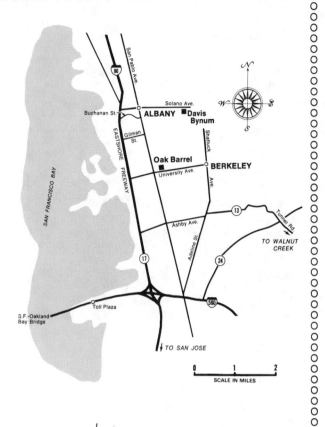

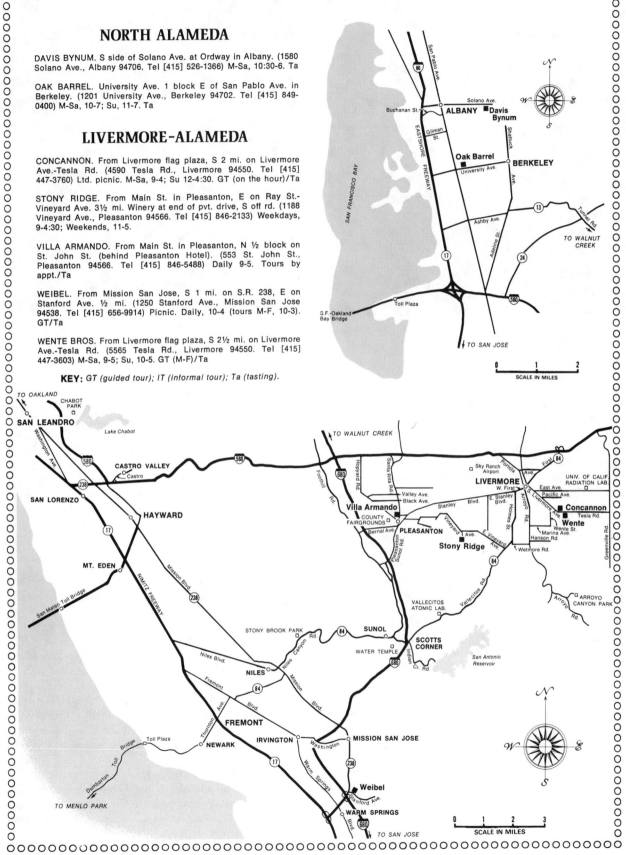

WENTE WINES wear steel jackets as they ferment out-doors. Glycol cooling controls temperatures.

PLEASANTON CHEESE factory has delights for small fry to compensate for dry spells in wineries.

Most of the gear is conventional, but students of wine-making will find some unusual fermentors to think about.

A man named Frank Garatti founded the winery in 1902 and expanded his premises off and on until 1937. In the main, Garatti wines were sold in bulk. A few carried the family name and were sold at the door.

As Villa Armando, the winery devotes itself to table wines: Chablis, Barbera, Burgundy, and Zinfandel, with emphasis on vintage-dated red wines. Several names on the Villa Armando list are not found elsewhere, Oro-bianco, Rubinello, Rustico all being proprietary types.

Miscellaneous Wineries. Pleasanton has a second winery site. Long known as Ruby Hill, it began a new life as Stony Ridge Winery when it was leased to partners Marc Berardinelli, Harry and Len Rosingana in 1975.

A man named John Crellen founded Ruby Hill in 1887. The property remained in the Crellen family until 1921, when Ernest Ferrario bought it. Ferrario owned Ruby Hill until 1973; then Southern Pacific Land Company became the official owner.

The founder had an eye for architecture. The brick and stone building, 60 by 185 feet and softened by a foreground of widely spaced trees, fulfills the romantic image of what a winery should be and still manages to make an individual impression.

Ernest Ferrario kept the property whole through thick and thin. Having launched himself into the wine trade in the midst of Prohibition, Ferrario did encounter some thin times.

Stony Ridge has a sizable vineyard connected to it. Some of the grapes will come from here and some from

farther away for such wines as Chardonnay, Johannis-berg Riesling, Semillon, Zinfandel, Zinfandel Nouveau, and Gamay. The winery has retail sales.

One other souvenir of the past is to be found in the region. The original Livermore vineyards of Cresta Blanca still exist on Arroyo Road near the veterans hospital even though the old winery has long been idle. (The name continues principally at a Mendocino County location where it is a subsidiary of Guild. See page 26.)

Other Than Wineries

Reliably warm and sunny, the Livermore Valley has spawned several picnic parks within easy reach of the wineries and vineyards.

Del Valle Regional Park, a part of the fine East Bay Regional Parks system, nestles in beautiful rolling hills around a large part of a reservoir lake's shoreline. It has abundant picnic sites in the shade of oaks, as well as swimming beaches and a boat launch (used, for the most part, by sailboaters and other quiet types). The park entrance is a bit more than 7 miles south of Tesla Road by way of Mines Road and Del Valle Road. The route, beginning midway between the Concannon and Wente wineries, is well signed.

A somewhat lower-key park is Arroyo Canyon, on the road that passes the old Cresta Blanca winery and the veterans hospital. The park nestles under trees along Arroyo Creek. It looks out on one vineyard and the grassy hills that frame Livermore. Arroyo Canyon Road starts in downtown Livermore as South L Street.

At Sunol, the San Francisco Water District maintains picnic tables and other comforts around its water temple. The entrance to the grounds is at the intersection of State Highway 21 with State Highway 84, just at the head of Niles Canyon. The location is ideal for persons dividing a day between the Livermore wineries and Weibel, at Warm Springs.

Pleasanton's main street has an early American flavor about it still, in spite of being ringed by endless contemporary housing tracts. The focal point is just west of St. John Street, where the landmark Pleasanton Hotel and the Pleasanton Cheese Factory face each other across the roadway. The cheese factory is a useful source of picnic foods to go with picnic wines acquired at the source.

The Alameda County Fair July 1-15 at Pleasanton, demonstrates that a good many cows remain in the area, but it also encompasses much more, including wine. The grounds are at the north side of the business district. The Livermore Rodeo, in early June, devotes itself wholly to cowboy arts.

Plotting a Route

The Livermore Valley has a pair of freeways crossing it. Interstate Highway 580 goes east-west; Interstate 680 runs north-south. One or the other will get a visitor into the region from almost anywhere at maximum speed.

Interstate 580 turns toward Livermore at Hayward near the east shore of San Francisco Bay and connects with Interstate 5 near the San Joaquin Valley town of Tracy. The road is scenic as it climbs up from the bay between steep hills. The first real vista from it, as you head east, is the Livermore Valley, which springs into full view just at the crest of a long rise. The second such panorama is the view of the Central Valley from the top of Altamont Pass.

The west hills leading toward Livermore are dark with scrub and trees, but the slopes ringing the valley have only grass on them. In dry summer their gold contrasts with the green of the approach and the green of the valley floor. From the east, the shift is less sharp. The climb up from Tracy is grassy gold even more than the descent into Livermore from Altamont.

Interstate 680 courses for most of its length in the shelter of the hills on the west side of the Livermore and connected valleys. The route begins at Martinez, on the bank of the Sacramento River, and ends at a junction with State Highway 17, on the southern boundary of Alameda County. It is useful for anyone launching a journey from Sacramento or beyond, or from San Jose or points south, as well as for those living along its roadway.

For the traveler heading up to Livermore from some point toward the south end of San Francisco Bay, State 84 from Newark or Mission San Jose offers a low-speed alternative to the interstate freeway.

The stretch from Mission San Jose-Niles to Sunol, also known as Niles Canyon Road, runs a course roughly parallel to the freeway but along the bottom of a twisting canyon. The best time to make use of Niles Canyon is on a hot summer day. It is full of eucalyptus trees that mightily perfume the still air. (The scent should get its greatest response from those who caught colds in the days when mothers doused pillows with eucalyptus oil, a sure cure.) The upper, eastern end of the canyon is at Sunol.

From Sunol to Livermore, the route continues to be a narrow, two-lane road designed to go around hills rather than through them. Aside from the Vallecitos atomic research station halfway along, all is pastures with recumbent oaks and grazing horses.

ALAMEDA COUNTY'S WEST SIDE

Alameda County's bay side had a substantial wine district in the Mission San Jose area before World War II and was a major district before World War I. In 1975, the roster of surviving vineyards and wineries in an urbanized landscape is very slim indeed.

The Wineries

One producing winery and a pair of winery-owned tasting rooms form a tenuous row from the south fringe of the county to the north edge.

Weibel Champagne Vineyards leans east into a steep and photogenic line of hills and looks west out over baylands at Warm Springs.

Look to the hills and time changes nothing on this south margin of Alameda County. Except for vine rows, the hand of man shows but little. Look the other way and the story is different. Westward in plain view lies an automobile assembly plant, which advertises itself as the world's largest building under one roof. It is the south end of an industrial-residential chain that runs unbroken to Oakland and beyond.

Being caught on the boundary between the worlds causes certain difficulties for the Weibels, but they go on in good humor at a winery that once belonged to Governor Leland Stanford.

Some of the buildings still would be recognizable to Stanford if he could stop by today, but the originals of 1869 have been supplemented since the Swiss family Weibel acquired the site in 1940. The winery is several hundred yards off State 238. The access road, bordered on one side by eucalyptus trees and on the other by olive trees, runs alongside the vineyard until it comes to the small adobe-style building which houses Weibel's tasting room. Just north of it, a long, low, red brick building houses all of the Champagne making and most of the stored still wines aging in bottle. Uphill from these are two rows of stainless steel aging tanks, the outdoor Sherry soleras, and the original winery building. A good deal of redwood and oak cooperage in it holds Weibel table

OLD AND NEW at Weibel. The puncheons hold sun-baked Sherries; the steel tanks are fermentors.

wines, most of them made at a new-in-1972 Weibel winery near Ukiah, in Mendocino County (see page 26), and transported to Mission San Jose for aging and bottling. Some wine is still made at Mission San Jose, the crusher being at the topmost level of the winery complex.

The brick Champagne building gives a clear view of the equipment for making both bottle-fermented and Charmat sparkling wines; this is one of the few cellars in which visitors can view a direct comparison and then go taste the results. The tasting room host pours sparkling wines of several sorts ranging from a Champagne Brut through a Charmat Sparkling Burgundy. The range of table wines encompasses nearly all of the generic and varietal types, and, finally, there are several appetizer and dessert wines. Weibel, unlike other wineries, chooses to make its Green Hungarian a fairly sweet table wine. Among its dessert types is a relatively unusual Black Muscat. A house specialty liqueur is called Tangor.

The Weibels have an arbor-shaded picnic table alongside the tasting room.

Davis Bynum Winery exists principally in the Russian River Valley of Sonoma County, but the tasting room is in Albany. The original winery tasting room on San Pablo Avenue moved in 1976 to Solano Avenue.

Proprietor Davis Bynum bought an old hop barn west of Windsor in 1972, converted it into a winery, and planted vineyards there. He had earlier made his wines from purchased grapes (and from the fruits of a small vineyard of his own in the Napa Valley) in a cellar behind the store front tasting room. His list of wines was, and still is, a longish one. The specialty of the house is

a jug wine called Barefoot Bynum. Most of the wines are varietal table wines, including Sauvignon Blanc, Traminer, Barbera, and Zinfandel.

Nearby, on University Avenue in downtown Berkeley, is Oak Barrel Cellars. The proprietors do not crush or ferment their own wines, but rather buy wines to age and blend. They offer tasting at the retail room.

Other Than Wineries

Mission San Jose, one of the chain of missions founded by the Franciscan community of Fra Serra, is only a mile or so north of Weibel Champagne Cellars and is open to visit. Architecturally, it is not the most imposing of the missions. The grounds behind have been preserved as they were in the late 1800s rather than in their original form. In sum, the property offers a clear impression of one of the busiest moments of local history.

Incidentally, the mission had the earliest vineyards in the district in the 1830s.

A tour of Alameda County wineries long enough to require a picnic would most likely include both Warm Springs and Livermore. The parks noted in the Livermore section (see page 54) would be the appropriate ones, with the San Francisco Water District park at Sunol being directly on the route.

Plotting a Route

State 17, the Nimitz Freeway, connects all the bayside towns of Alameda County and is the expedient way to get into the neighborhood of either Weibel or Bynum from most of the San Francisco Bay region.

Interstate 680 courses quickly between Pleasanton and Warm Springs, linking the Livermore Valley wineries with Weibel. A slower, more bucolic route is old State 84, which ambles through dry hills for a time and then down tree-filled Niles Canyon as it goes from Pleasanton to Warm Springs.

 ## CONTRA COSTA COUNTY

Contra Costa County contains only two wineries active at the moment. Contra Costa County has seldom had many more wineries than two and at this point is urbanizing at a rate which suggests a continuation of that condition. The county east of the hills cupping San Francisco Bay still has a great amount of open space, but little or none of it has been devoted to grapes for climatic or other good reasons.

The Wineries

The two wineries persist in the midst of Martinez's more pervasive petroleum industry. They are a mile or so apart on the southeast side of town.

J. E. Digardi Winery goes back a good way in Martinez history, to 1886. The city has come to engulf the old property, which at this point has a small retail store alongside Pacheco Boulevard, the fine frame house and winery behind that, and the lone remaining acre of vines still farther to the rear, running to the crest of a small slope.

It is a pleasing scene but limited by industrial establishments on either side.

The Digardi family persists at this point in making a certain amount of table wine, but it has passed the day of regular tours and tasting. Digardi Gamay, Zinfandel, and others of the list of table wines can be bought at the retail store.

Conrad Viano Winery, on an edge of Martinez, has much of the air of a country winery. The family home has a rear corner of the basement set aside for tasting and retail sales. Three other smallish buildings of painted concrete block are behind that and slightly downhill. They are the winery and storage buildings.

Beyond, on the upslope, several acres of vineyard look back at the clustered structures (and several neighboring residences).

There is not enough gear on hand to call for a guided tour. A few minutes' poking about will reveal the crusher and press at the back of the backmost building and an array of small redwood upright tanks inside of it. Otherwise the scene is mostly farm tools and stored cases.

The tasting room takes longer. The Vianos have under their well-designed label Barbera, Burgundy, Cabernet Sauvignon, Gamay, Zinfandel (which they prize), Zinfandel Rosé, Chablis, Grey Riesling, and, among appetizer and dessert types, Muscatel, Port, and Sherry. Sales are recorded on a small pad; change comes from a pint jar which otherwise might have gone to hold the honey sold as a sideline.

It is a busy jar. The family bought the vineyard in 1920, founded the winery in 1946, and had to build a bigger cellar in 1967 and an addition in 1971. The third generation of Vianos is at work today.

There is a picnic site alongside the vines for those who would tarry over a bird and a bottle.

Other Than Wineries

The tiny, waterside town of Port Costa once was a teeming Sacramento River port. Bridges and other aspects of progress caused it to become technologically unemployed in the 1930s.

Its stout stone buildings, busy again since the 1960s with restaurants and dealers in a variety of used goods, have become highly visitable relics of an earlier day.

In character, the town matches the nearby wineries to a fine degree. Together they make a complete day of looking into the past.

Port Costa is just off State 4 a few minutes downstream from Martinez.

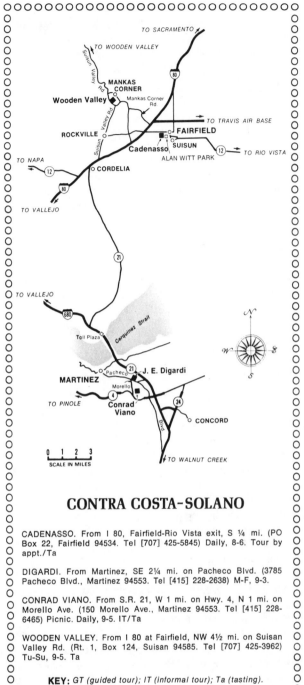

CONTRA COSTA-SOLANO

CADENASSO. From I 80, Fairfield-Rio Vista exit, S ¼ mi. (PO Box 22, Fairfield 94534. Tel [707] 425-5845) Daily, 8-6. Tour by appt./Ta

DIGARDI. From Martinez, SE 2¼ mi. on Pacheco Blvd. (3785 Pacheco Blvd., Martinez 94553. Tel [415] 228-2638) M-F, 9-3.

CONRAD VIANO. From S.R. 21, W 1 mi. on Hwy. 4, N 1 mi. on Morello Ave. (150 Morello Ave., Martinez 94553. Tel [415] 228-6465) Picnic. Daily, 9-5. IT/Ta

WOODEN VALLEY. From I 80 at Fairfield, NW 4½ mi. on Suisan Valley Rd. (Rt. 1, Box 124, Suisan 94585. Tel [707] 425-3962) Tu-Su, 9-5. Ta

KEY: GT (guided tour); IT (informal tour); Ta (tasting).

Plotting a Route

Interstate 680, the freeway that splits Contra Costa County north and south, terminates just on the south side of Martinez. Combined with State 24 (a freeway) from Oakland to Walnut Creek, it is a reasonable way to get there from San Francisco and other points south around the bay.

An alternative is Interstate 80 (Eastshore Freeway) from Oakland to Pinole, then State 4 (the Arnold Highway) east to Martinez. In general this is slower and a bit less scenic, but it does pass Port Costa closely.

From the north, State 21 connects Cordelia on Interstate 80 with Martinez.

SOLANO COUNTY

Habitually, Solano County is appended to Napa to form a single wine district. The statistical reasons might be sound, but traveling from one county to the other does not go half so quickly as a trip between Solano and Contra Costa County. For this reason Solano here is attached to the region east of San Francisco Bay.

Specifically, it is only 21 miles — 25 minutes — from Fairfield to Martinez by State 21, a four-lane freeway, but it is 45 miles — an hour or more — from Fairfield to St. Helena over an admixture of state and county two-lane roads.

The Wineries

Only two wineries operate in Solano County at present, a producing one in Fairfield and a wine cellar northwest of the town.

Cadenasso Winery is the producing one. The ivy-darkened concrete block walls of the main building are visible to motorists on Interstate 80 just as they approach the Fairfield–Rio Vista–State 12 exit ramp on the west side of Fairfield. Inside, an eclectic collection of oak ovals and small redwood uprights marches in four close ranks from one end to the other.

The tasting room, in the cellar beneath owner Frank Cadenasso's home, has as its entry an arched concrete tunnel. Downstairs the walls are mostly painted a vivid pink to match the company stationery.

Cadenasso began in 1906 when father Giovanni Cadenasso planted vines north of Cordelia. It continued when he moved to Fairfield to plant vines across the street from the present winery. That vineyard became county hospital grounds after the senior Cadenasso sold the land and dismantled the winery as a sensible response to Prohibition. The present site dates from 1926 (the main building came later, in 1942).

Cadenasso wines, served for tasting with great pride but no pretense, include Chenin Blanc, Grey Riesling, Chablis, and Sauterne among whites; Burgundy, Cabernet Sauvignon, Grignolino, Pinot Noir, and Zinfandel among the reds. The Zinfandel and all of the generics can be had in jugs as well as fifths, and a considerable part of each day's sale goes out the door in the generous gallon container.

Ordinarily there are no tours. A look through the winery requires an appointment, very nearly the only formality Cadenasso allows, let alone asks. The staff is too small, though, to lay down its work without planning ahead for visitors.

Wooden Valley Winery is of the same degree of informality as Cadenasso. Its proprietor is named Mario Lanza. (This one does not sing particularly well.)

There is no tour at Wooden Valley. The tasting and sales room is one of four frame buildings grouped around a sizable courtyard, but that one is unmistakable. On weekends, especially, the court is full of parked automobiles and the tasting room full of local patrons exchanging empty jugs for full ones.

The wines on hand include several generic table wines (in fifths and jugs) and a broad spectrum of varietals in fifths only. A complete list of appetizer and dessert wines is also there to be tasted. Sparkling wines are not offered for tasting.

Other Than Wineries

Solano County offers no great abundance of picnic parks or other recreational diversions close to its wineries.

One exception, directly next to the Cadenasso Winery on West Texas Street, is Alan Witt Park, a spaciously arranged collection of playgrounds and picnic lawns.

Plotting a Route

Interstate 80 is the obvious means of getting to Fairfield from either Sacramento or the San Francisco Bay region. It is all freeway except for 2 or 3 miles at most.

State 12, though not freeway, offers a fairly direct route east to Lodi or west to Napa.

State 21, as mentioned, connects with Martinez in a great hurry. The road slips along the flat, just at the base of a pleasing range of low hills from Cordelia all the way to the river bank, where the Suisun mothball fleet provides a wistful vista.

But these are mainly means of getting somewhere. The joys of driving in this part of the world belong with Suisun Valley Road, Wooden Valley Road, State 121 from Cordelia to Lake Berryessa (and on across into the Napa Valley if time does not weigh heavily), and whatever connecting roads seem promising on the spot.

The Suisun and Wooden valleys, both small, look fine in all seasons. They even smell good early in March when their abundant orchards bloom a fragrant cloud of white and pink above carpets of indelibly yellow mustard and beneath canopies of blue sky.

The hills west, in this season, are bright green with new grass and dull green with old oaks.

These are old roads, narrow and curving. Summer drivers bustle along in hopes of finding some cooler place; but in late winter or early spring when the weather is balmy, some of them tend to grow forgetful of their goals. On such days the wheels of progress grind as slowly as those of justice, but the views are exceedingly fine.

CALIFORNIA WINE CHART

DINNER WINES

VARIETALS
Named for the grapes from which they are made

WHITE WINES

Light crisp white wines, pale golden or slightly green gold in color. Most are pleasantly dry. Some (*) may have a hint of sweetness.

*Emerald Riesling	Johannisberg Riesling
*Gewürztraminer	(White Riesling)
*Green Hungarian	Sylvaner
Grey Riesling	Traminer

Rich, fuller-flavored wines. These are usually dry wines, straw to light golden in color. Some may have a hint of sweetness.

Chardonnay	Dry Semillon
(Pinot Chardonnay)	Pinot Blanc
*Chenin Blanc (White Pinot)	*Sauvignon Blanc

Medium to pronounced sweetness in these wines, often served with dessert rather than dinner.

Malvasia Bianca	Muscat Canelli
Muscat Bordelaise	Sweet Semillon

ROSÉ WINES

These are light, fruity wines, sometimes dry, sometimes slightly sweet (*), with a pink color ranging in tone from deep rose to a pale, orange-tinted hue.

Cabernet Rosé	Grignolino Rosé
Gamay Rosé	Zinfandel Rosé
*Grenache Rosé	

RED WINES

Fresh, fruity red wines, dry and aromatic, light to medium body.

Cabernet	Pinot St. George
Gamay	(Red Pinot)
Gamay Beaujolais	Ruby Cabernet
Grignolino	Zinfandel

Rich red wines with distinctive flavor and appealing ruby color, medium to full in body.

Barbera	Petite Sirah
Cabernet Sauvignon	Pinot Noir
Charbono	

GENERICS
Named for wines with similar characteristics, usually for the district of origin

WHITE WINES

Light, medium-dry white wines ranging in color from pale golden to slightly green gold.

Rhine Wine	White Chianti

Rich, distinctive wines with full flavor and a pale or light gold color. These wines are dry, often fruity.

Chablis	Dry Sauterne	Mountain White

Medium-sweet to quite sweet wines, often served with dessert rather than dinner.

Haut Sauterne	Sweet Sauterne
Light Muscat	"Chateau" white wines

ROSÉ WINES

These wines are light, fruity, usually medium-dry.

Vin Rosé	Rosé

RED WINES

Dry wines, from light red to deep ruby in color, often pleasantly tart, with medium to full body.

Burgundy	Claret
Chianti	Mountain Red

Mellow reds, of medium body with just a touch of sweetness and a pleasing, hearty flavor.

Barberone	Vino Rosso

PROPRIETARIES: Other red, white, and rosé dinner wines are labeled with special names selected by the winemaker. These proprietary names usually are coined words with descriptive value. Proprietary wines parallel generics in range and use.

APPETIZER WINES

Sherry (Cocktail, Dry, Medium-Dry)
Vermouth (Dry, Sweet)

SPECIAL NATURAL WINES: These are grape wines flavored with fruit juices or natural essences. Citrus flavors are especially popular, also mint, coffee, chocolate, several herbs. Most carry coined names.

SPARKLING WINES

Champagne (Natural—very dry; Brut—dry; Extra Dry—a hint of sweetness; Dry—medium sweet; Sec—noticeably sweet; Demi-Sec—very sweet)
Rosé (Pink Champagne, Crackling Rosé)
Red (Sparkling Burgundy)
Muscat (Sparkling Muscat)

DESSERT WINES

Angelica	Port (Ruby, Tawny,
Cream Sherry	Tinta, White)
Madeira	Tokay
Marsala	

Muscatel (Black Muscat; Muscat Frontignan; Muscatel, gold or red)

CENTRAL COAST

A district of great change and great vinous variety

The Central Coast counties of California are in a curiously unbalanced state at present. Although most of the vines grow in Monterey and others of the more southerly counties, most of the visitable wineries are in Santa Clara and others of the more northerly counties.

The urban pressures that began to be inexorable on vineyards early in the 1960s will, no doubt, weigh ever more on wineries through the 1970s. In the meantime, students who wish to see both vine and wine at the source have an enormous territory to consider when they go looking at such as Almaden, Paul Masson, Mirassou, and their like in this divided region.

The north side of Santa Clara County, where commercial winegrowing got its start south of San Francisco Bay, has been heavily urbanized since the late 1950s. Though vines almost have disappeared, this remains a focal point for wineries.

The south half of the county was and remains a center for country jug wines.

Monterey County now supports a tremendous majority of the region's vineyards but is just beginning to show wineries to go with the grapes.

Woven into the region as minor but estimable contributors to the vinous character of the Central Coast are Santa Cruz, San Benito, and San Luis Obispo counties.

U.S. Highway 101 slices straight down the length of the region, from San Jose at the north to San Luis Obispo at the south, a distance of more than 150 miles. In every part of the region, wineries welcome visitors. A serious student would require at least a week to cover all the ground. More time would be better. Those with the advantage that comes with living on the spot can divide up the territory enough to spend many weekends poking into all the possibilities.

NORTH SANTA CLARA

Since homes and freeways and shopping centers have come to occupy most of the local flatlands, northern Santa Clara County's few vines and many wineries have retreated into the hills, both east and west of the valley floor.

All but one of the wineries are to the west, where the hills rise sharply to average elevations of 1,800 feet, screening out enough sea fog to make grape growing possible only a few miles from the Pacific Ocean shore.

The Wineries

Santa Clara's wineries run an amazing gamut from miniature to very large. The smallest ones are the most remote; the largest, the reverse. Both sorts form a reasonably tight chain from Cupertino down to Los Gatos, with only one or two stray links away from the main concentration.

Almaden Vineyards dates back to 1852, counting its shared ancestry with Paul Masson.

Its founders were two Frenchmen named Etienne

VAST VINEYARD of Almaden rolls upslope and down the far side in pioneer San Benito County district.

Thee and Charles LeFranc, who planted vines on the site of the present Almaden Home Winery in Los Gatos. LeFranc, having married a Thee daughter, watched history recycle. LeFranc's daughter married his eventual junior partner, Paul Masson. (Masson later founded his own firm; the original Thee-LeFranc property continued in other hands.)

These days, Thee and LeFranc are but remote ancestors in Almaden's family tree. San Jose has grown to surround the original winery, where ranks and files of vines have largely been replaced by ranks and files of tract homes. This last has not wrought great improvements in the scenery, though Almaden has retained enough vineyard on the Home Winery property to keep it handsome.

While the suburbs have been growing up around the original winery, Almaden has been growing up in several other places. The company has two producing wineries south of Hollister in San Benito County, a third winery at Kingsburg in the San Joaquin Valley, and a warehouse for bottled wines on the southern fringes of San Jose.

Almaden welcomes visitors in two differing ways at two differing places.

The original winery property on Blossom Hill Road serves now as a bottling arena and sparkling wine cellar. Open to view is a highly efficient bottling operation — one of the largest and fastest in the state. As a prelude, tourists can have a look at a museum of Almaden's long and colorful history.

To taste the wines, one must go to the village of San Jaun Bautista, in San Benito County. At one corner of the plaza of this historic stage stop, Almaden has installed a pleasant little building where it offers its remarkably wide range of wines for tasting and sale. (The producing wineries, some miles to the south, are not open to tour, but a drive past gives a fair impression of the scope of the company's winemaking operations, as well as some superb vineyard panoramas. The winery on Cienega Road devotes itself primarily to reds. The one just off State Highway 156 at Paicines produces whites.)

David Bruce is up in the hills a couple of miles southwest of Los Gatos on Bear Creek Road. A visit to the winery ties in neatly to excursions to either northern Santa Clara or Santa Cruz counties' wineries.

Bruce launched his winery in 1964, completing a sizable concrete block cellar building in 1968. A physician, he makes Chardonnay, White Riesling, Grenache, Petite Sirah, and Zinfandel as a second profession. Most of the grapes come from his own mountainous vineyards.

There is neither tour nor tasting except by appointment. With appointment, Bruce will lead visitors around his vineyards just west of Summit Road and through the winemaking operation from start to finish.

Gemello Winery, hidden away behind a bowling alley on El Camino Real in Mountain View, dates from 1934, when the neighborhood consisted of orchards.

Founder John Gemello worked for the original Montebello Wine Company in Cupertino at the time and

VISITORS to Mission San Juan Bautista can sample wines at adjacent Almaden tasting room.

the outside may strike the eye of its beholder, the inside is an efficient winery and has much to recommend it to visitors. A raised walkway permits bird's-eye views of an expanse of handsome cooperage (glass-lined steel, oak ovals, and redwood uprights all nestled together in harmony), three model bottling lines, and all the steps in Champagne making, including huge stacks of the sparkling wine fermenting in bottles.

Masson, in fact, offers one of few chances to study what is called the transfer process of Champagne making. The lesson is clearly presented. Guides conduct tours every few minutes.

The building was completed in 1959 (then expanded in 1967) long after Masson's owners had decided to move the main body of vineyards south, so no wine is crushed at this site. All crushing goes on at Pinnacles in Monterey County (where a new producing winery was completed only a few days before the 1966 harvest began) or, to a much smaller degree, at the Mountain Winery.

But Saratoga is where all Masson wine comes for final aging, bottling, and packaging, and this is where it is at hand for sampling in a spacious and comfortably appointed tasting hall. Masson makes a great many wines: nearly all of the familiar varietal and generic table wines, their several sparkling wines, and a good many appetizer and dessert types.

Of late, Masson has adopted a policy of offering specialties. The prime examples are a white wine called Emerald Dry, two reds called Rubion and Baroque, and a dessert wine called Madiera.

Music lovers now have the greatest reason to visit (for summer concerts) the original home of Paul Masson wines — the Mountain Winery, several miles west into the hills above Saratoga.

The winery on the hill clings to every architectural tradition the Champagne Cellar does not. Built of stone, it was nestled into the hillside so gravity could do most of the work of moving wines before pumps were harnessed to motors. The building has had its literal ups and downs since the flesh-and-blood Paul Masson had the winery built in 1880. It had to be rebuilt after the earthquake of 1906, at which time it acquired its churchly front from a ruined chapel in San Jose. It had to be rebuilt yet a second time after a gutting fire in 1941. (The old man did not have to deal with the fire. He had died a year earlier after 58 years of winemaking in California and 4 years of retirement.)

The crusher still operates in season, but mainly the old winery serves as an aging cellar for small casks of dessert wine (including some experimental ones), and as the site for two concert series. Music at the Vineyards, an institution since 1958, offers chamber music on selected weekends in June, July, and August. The newer Vintage Sounds series begins when the classical one ends, offering jazz and folk music.

Tickets and information can be obtained by writing Music at the Vineyards, P.O. Box 97, Saratoga, CA

started his own winery as a hobby. It has been more durable than Montebello. John Gemello's son Mario assumed control in the early 1940s and found the enterprise so active that he was required to add a good deal of oak to the existing supply of cooperage. Mario is the winemaker. His partner on the business side is Louis Sarto.

Although the focus is on the red varietals Cabernet Sauvignon, Pinot Noir, Barbera, Zinfandel, and Petite Sirah, white wines are also to be found on the list at Gemello's.

The retail store adjoining the winery sells all the wines. Since the winery building is so small that a tour would consist mainly of getting to the middle of the room and looking around the edges, formal tours do not exist. But the proprietors will let visitors who make appointments have a look at the inner workings.

Paul Masson Champagne and Wine Cellar spreads out as widely as Almaden does. For visitors, though, things are centralized at the big complex of buildings on the valley floor just east of Saratoga.

As its photograph shows, Paul Masson departs completely from traditional winery architecture. However

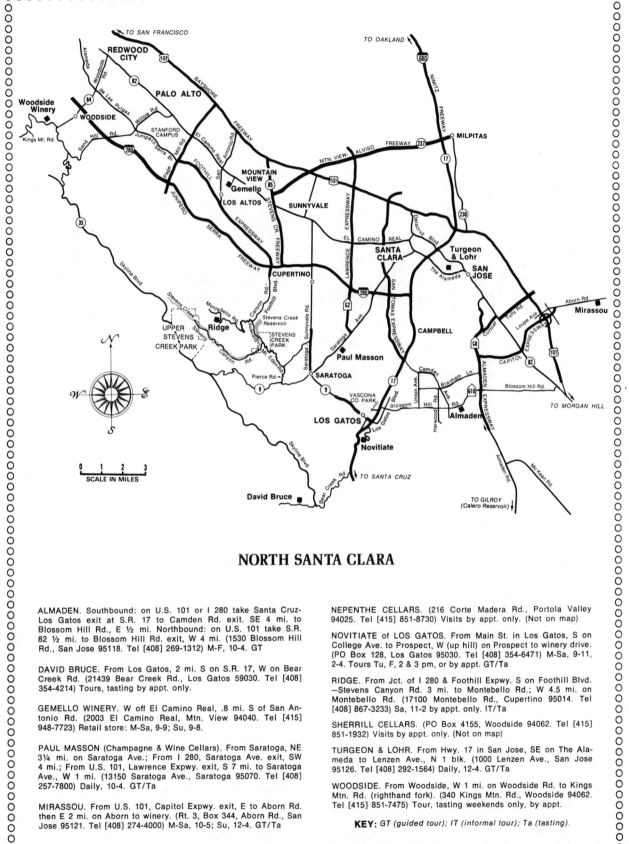

NORTH SANTA CLARA

ALMADEN. Southbound: on U.S. 101 or I 280 take Santa Cruz-Los Gatos exit at S.R. 17 to Camden Rd. exit. SE 4 mi. to Blossom Hill Rd., E ½ mi. Northbound: on U.S. 101 take S.R. 82 ½ mi. to Blossom Hill Rd. exit, W 4 mi. (1530 Blossom Hill Rd., San Jose 95118. Tel [408] 269-1312) M-F, 10-4. GT

DAVID BRUCE. From Los Gatos, 2 mi. S on S.R. 17, W on Bear Creek Rd. (21439 Bear Creek Rd., Los Gatos 59030. Tel [408] 354-4214) Tours, tasting by appt. only.

GEMELLO WINERY. W off El Camino Real, .8 mi. S of San Antonio Rd. (2003 El Camino Real, Mtn. View 94040. Tel [415] 948-7723) Retail store: M-Sa, 9-9; Su, 9-8.

PAUL MASSON (Champagne & Wine Cellars). From Saratoga, NE 3¼ mi. on Saratoga Ave.; From I 280, Saratoga Ave. exit, SW 4 mi.; From U.S. 101, Lawrence Expwy. exit, S 7 mi. to Saratoga Ave., W 1 mi. (13150 Saratoga Ave., Saratoga 95070. Tel [408] 257-7800) Daily, 10-4. GT/Ta

MIRASSOU. From U.S. 101, Capitol Expwy. exit, E to Aborn Rd. then E 2 mi. on Aborn to winery. (Rt. 3, Box 344, Aborn Rd., San Jose 95121. Tel [408] 274-4000) M-Sa, 10-5; Su, 12-4. GT/Ta

NEPENTHE CELLARS. (216 Corte Madera Rd., Portola Valley 94025. Tel [415] 851-8730) Visits by appt. only. (Not on map)

NOVITIATE of LOS GATOS. From Main St. in Los Gatos, S on College Ave. to Prospect, W (up hill) on Prospect to winery drive. (PO Box 128, Los Gatos 95030. Tel [408] 354-6471) M-Sa, 9-11, 2-4. Tours Tu, F, 2 & 3 pm, or by appt. GT/Ta

RIDGE. From Jct. of I 280 & Foothill Expwy. S on Foothill Blvd. —Stevens Canyon Rd. 3 mi. to Montebello Rd.; W 4.5 mi. on Montebello Rd. (17100 Montebello Rd., Cupertino 95014. Tel [408] 867-3233) Sa, 11-2 by appt. only. IT/Ta

SHERRILL CELLARS. (PO Box 4155, Woodside 94062. Tel [415] 851-1932) Visits by appt. only. (Not on map)

TURGEON & LOHR. From Hwy. 17 in San Jose, SE on The Alameda to Lenzen Ave., N 1 blk. (1000 Lenzen Ave., San Jose 95126. Tel [408] 292-1564) Daily, 12-4. GT/Ta

WOODSIDE. From Woodside, W 1 mi. on Woodside Rd. to Kings Mtn. Rd. (righthand fork). (340 Kings Mtn. Rd., Woodside 94062. Tel [415] 851-7475) Tour, tasting weekends only, by appt.

KEY: GT (guided tour); IT (informal tour); Ta (tasting).

PERFECTLY MODERN Paul Masson Champagne Cellars offers clear demonstrations of table wine aging, along with lessons on making of Masson sparkling wines. The tasting hall allows visitors to sample both.

95070; or, for Vintage Sounds, by writing to Browne Vintners, 505 Beach Street, San Francisco, CA 94133.

Only for these concerts is the winery open to the public.

Mirassou Vineyards, coming now into the hands of its owning family's fifth generation, has one of the oldest names in Santa Clara winemaking, though the label is a relative newcomer in retail stores.

A French vineyardist, Pierre Pellier, established the dynasty in 1854 in what is now downtown San Jose. (Following an earlier exploratory visit in 1848, he then returned to France to gather a wife and thousands of vine cuttings.) Subsequently another Frenchman, Pierre Mirassou, met and married a Pellier daughter. That was in 1881. The name Mirassou has figured in California vintages since.

An old photo on the tasting room wall shows wooden tank trucks loading Mirassou wines into railroad cars for the long voyage east in the era before World War I. After the enforced respite of Prohibition, the third and fourth generations resumed winemaking, again anonymously. This time, though, the Mirassous embarked on the unique course of making varietal wines for sale in bulk to other California wineries.

As late as 1968, it still took a bit of a pilgrimage to find wine under the Mirassou label. It was sold only at the winery, located after a long string of stoplights south of San Jose.

Now, with the fifth generation firmly embarked on a path of family identity with family vintages, it is possible to find Mirassou wines at retail shops all across the country. But the winery remains a good place to go looking for them. In fact, it's a good deal easier journey than it used to be, owing to U.S. 101's upgrading to freeway status.

The main winery building, with a richly appointed tasting room in one front corner, is a squarely built, solid masonry building nestled into the beginnings of a steep slope southeast of San Jose. Once, not so many years ago, it was the whole winery. Now it holds only a small proportion of the aging cooperage and a bottling line. A second building just uphill holds most of the oak barrels and the Champagne cellar; a third building at the rear stores the bottled wines. (A fourth building a couple of miles away holds much of the large wooden cooperage.)

Outdoors, at the rear of the original cellar, is a complex assemblage of crushers and steel fermenting tanks. (Though the equipment hardly looks it, the whole array is portable. Most Mirassou grapevines are in the Salinas Valley of Monterey County. Anticipating having to move the whole winery operation there one day, the family has done its best to be ready.)

Pending the move south, this is one of Santa Clara's most instructive wineries for visit, especially during the October-November harvest season. The main works are out in the open enough for sidewalk superintending to

CHAMPAGNE – HOW THE BUBBLES GET THERE

Sparkling wine dates from the time of Dom Perignon, a Benedictine monk who made wine for l'Abbaye d'Hautvillers in the late 1600s.

In a sense effervescing wine had long since invented itself, and Perignon only invented suitable bottles and stoppers for keeping the bubbles in.

His original method was chancy. It involved starting a secondary fermentation in the tightly corked bottle and hoping that total CO_2 would not explode the glass. One scholar has it that the odds ran no better than 60-40 on any bottle in those pioneer years. (Fermentation is the conversion of sugar by yeast into roughly equal parts of CO_2 and alcohol; the early cellarkeepers took a relaxed view of the interrelationship between sugar and eventual gas pressure.)

Now, with refined measurements, the same technique is still used and called *la methode Champenoise.* The Champagne master blends still wines to his taste, bottles them, and adds a mixture of sugar and yeast before capping each bottle. This mixture produces the secondary fermentation. After it has finished its work, the mixture falls as sediment and is worked into the neck of the bottle. Then the neck is frozen in brine or other solution so the sediment can pop out as a plug of ice (aided by an average gas pressure of 100 pounds per square inch). Next is added dosage, a syrup that governs the sweetness of the finished wine. The final cork is wired into place. After a period of rest, the wine is ready to market.

Latterly, science has added some variations. One is the German method called Carstens Transfer Process. It starts out in the same way as *methode Champenoise.* But when it comes time to remove the sediment, the bottles are emptied under pressure into a holding tank, the wine is filtered and is then returned to bottles with the desired dosage. Another method, French in origin, is called Charmat or Bulk Process. In this case the wine undergoes its secondary fermentation in a glass-lined tank rather than in bottles. Then, as in the Carstens method, it is filtered on its way to bottles.

A great many California wineries make sparkling wines. Most have tours. Among the clearest demonstrations: Korbel, Hanns Kornell, and Schramsberg for *methode Champenoise;* Weibel for that and Charmat; The Christian Brothers (Greystone) for Charmat; and Paul Masson for transfer process.

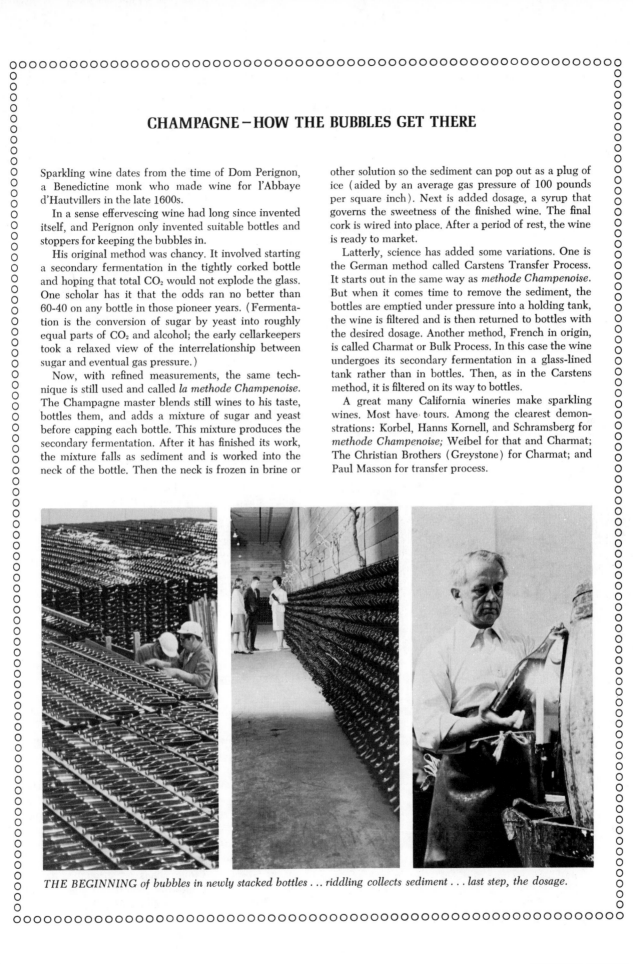

THE BEGINNING of bubbles in newly stacked bottles . . . riddling collects sediment . . . last step, the dosage.

be easy. The cellars hold every kind of cooperage, as well as a highly traditional Champagne making set-up.

The resulting wines can be tasted in relaxed comfort. The roster includes Chenin Blanc, Gewürztraminer, Johannisberg Riesling, and Monterey Riesling among whites, and Cabernet Sauvignon, Petite Sirah, Pinot Noir, and Zinfandel among reds.

The Novitiate of Los Gatos has few peers for handsome setting. The winery building cuts into a narrow shelf halfway up a hill of some size. As they approach Los Gatos, drivers westbound on State 17 or southbound on Monte Sereno Road can see the white winery and, on the crest above it, the vineyards.

Within the winery building, amid observable outlines of still older buildings, dim tunnels lead off in several directions. There is no telling the age of some of the oak casks that line the tunnels. The Novitiate has been making sacramental wines since 1888 and has acquired cooperage as opportunity has allowed. Some casks came without pedigree papers.

But not all is cobwebby romance. The Jesuit fathers who run the winery are an experimental lot. They have an early-model continuous press on hand that is satisfactory for making the beginnings of brandy but not much else. A since-reassigned winemaker-priest designed and installed a battery of highly efficient stainless steel fermenting tanks after having studied on the subject at U.C. Davis. Both presses and fermentors are on the uphill side of the building.

Down in one of the deeper regions stands a stainless steel tank shaped somewhat after the fashion of a Mercury space capsule and equipped with a porthole. In view inside is the flor culture used in the Novitiate Dry Sherry. (Other flor cultures crop up throughout the winery in a wild variety of bottles, flagons, and demijohns. The winemaker waits patiently to see if variant strains might develop.)

Getting around to see all of this involves a considerable amount of climbing spidery iron stairways, since the office building is at the lowest level and the start of the tour is at the highest, and there is no alternate route. At the end of the tour, the tasting room is in one of the cellars where table, appetizer, and dessert wines are offered for leisurely consideration.

The winery is closed to visitors on Sundays and on legal and church holidays.

Ridge Vineyards, started as a weekend hobby early in the 1960s, has been growing steadily ever since. At this point the business has long since gone beyond the hobby stage. There is enough Ridge to fill the original building and a much larger second cellar.

Ridge's two locations, almost a mile apart, are both spectacular. The name comes from the fact that the winery does indeed sit on a ridge due west of Cupertino. The topmost vineyard yields views out to the Pacific Ocean and down into a vast portion of San Francisco Bay. The rest of the premises do not lag far off that scenic pace.

Visitors with reservations are welcomed Saturdays at the rustic original winery, now a bottling and case storage building. It is hidden in a little fold 100 yards or so off Monte Bello Ridge Road. (Drivers need to watch mailbox numbers carefully for the cue to angle left into a dirt drive that, from the road, appears to have no purpose.)

When the weather is reasonably good, tasting and talking go on outdoors, at one edge of a small patch of vines, but there is indoor space for gloomy days.

From time to time the hosts are moved to cart visitors up to the producing winery, a handsome old frame building that covers a sizable cellar dug into the stone hillside. The equipment is modern, but the building goes back to the turn of the century, when it housed the Montebello Winery.

The labels on Ridge wines are probably the most explicit of any in California. The list of labels is dominated by Cabernet Sauvignon and Zinfandel but also includes Chardonnay and White Riesling.

JESUIT FATHER makes regular rounds at Novitiate of Los Gatos winery, checking hundreds of oak barrels.

Turgeon & Lohr has its brick-front winery in San Jose and its vineyards in Monterey County.

The winery opened to the public in 1976.

A tasting room of redwood walls and ceiling has been set inside one end of the building. Tours begin here. The staff explains the winemaking procedures, not necessarily in order, when time permits.

The owners are Bernard Turgeon, Jerry Lohr, and winemaker Peter Stern. The wines, including the proprietary Jade, Rosé of Cabernet Sauvignon, Petite Sirah, Chenin Blanc, and Cabernet Sauvignon, carry the label name J. Lohr. There are also several generics.

Miscellaneous Wineries. The Santa Cruz Mountains — in San Mateo, Santa Clara, and Santa Cruz counties — long have held a fascination for people who make small quantities of wine with great intensity of feeling; there is nothing to call these winemakers but semiprofessionals. In all cases, the proprietors have brought money from other occupations to support their wee wineries or else continue to work at regular jobs while they make wine.

A man named Martin Ray managed, from 1943 onward, to create vast interest in a very small winery high in the hills east of Saratoga. He died in 1975.

Before his death the property was divided. A new owner now operates the Ray winery; a second winery, Mt. Eden, is operated by a consortium of vineyard owners with winemaker Merry Edwards. The principal varieties in the vineyards are Chardonnay, Cabernet Sauvignon, and Pinot Noir.

The property never was large enough to allow casual visits. Now neither of the two properties is large enough to accept any visitors other than friends of the owners.

Woodside Vineyards was founded by Robert and Polly Mullen in 1960 and bonded in 1963, but its legacy is a long and rich one. The Cabernet Sauvignon vineyard is on a part of the old and even legendary LaQuesta Vineyard of E. H. Rixford. (Its palmiest years were the 1880s, when wines from it commanded the highest prices of that era.) The Mullens have revived the La-Questa label for Cabernet Sauvignon but use Woodside on Chardonnay, Chenin Blanc, and Pinot Noir.

Vineyards and winery are just west of Woodside town.

A nearby neighbor, G. L. Burtness, produces a minute annual volume of wine under the Nepenthe label. Yet another tiny winery in the Woodside-Portola Valley neighborhood is Sherrill Cellars, owned by Nathaniel and Jan Sherrill.

All of these require specific appointments for visits.

Other Than Wineries

Urban distractions abound in the neighborhood to the same degree they abound in Alameda County or in the Cucamonga district. These notes cover only one or two with historic ties to wine, and some potential picnic sites.

Leland Stanford in his day ranked as one of the

MASONRY WALLS of upper cellar at Mirassou house sparkling wines. A twin building holds table wines.

state's most enthusiastic winegrowers, although the histories suggest his skills did not come anywhere near matching his hopes. Skilled or not, he established three major wineries, one of them on the north side of the present Stanford University campus. The handsome brick building still stands between the Stanford Shopping Center and the university's hospital. Shops and restaurants fill it now.

Farther south, the Mission Santa Clara has similarly dim ties to the vine. Santa Clara is something of a curiosity piece because of the fact that vines did not prosper there during the mission era. The failure mystified the mission fathers but has been cleared up since. Santa Clara is too cool for the Mission variety to ripen properly. It was one of the earliest hints at the complexity of microclimate zones in the northern coast counties.

The mission adjoins the campus of Santa Clara University on the Alameda.

The associated wineries of Santa Clara Valley maintain an information booth in Los Gatos for tourists in the region at Old Town, a restaurant and shopping complex just off the main street. Signs point the way.

For picnickers, Stevens Creek Park, a long strip along a narrow and shaded creek, offers picnic sites aplenty in

OLD TOWN in Los Gatos is an arcade of specialty shops.

VASONA PARK in Los Gatos offers diverse recreation.

March or April. But as spring wears into summer, the park begins to be crowded. Shallow as it is, the creek is a fine playground for children, and that accounts for a good part of the traffic. The sheltered and wooded nature of the place contributes the rest of the allure.

The park is west of Cupertino on the same road that leads to Ridge Vineyards.

Vasona Lake County Park straddles a creek and reservoir directly alongside State 17 at Los Gatos. It has abundant picnic and recreation facilities on well-kept lawns.

Just west of Los Gatos, where the coast ranges begin to climb, Lexington Reservoir's shoreline is a developed picnic and water sports park — but a less manicured one than Vasona.

Plotting a Route

The main thing in winery touring is to get in tune with the subject. This calls more for curving excursions through back country than for flat trajectory flights on freeways. Built up though it is, northern Santa Clara County still has a few back roads.

To get a day in the Saratoga-Cupertino-Los Gatos district off to a bucolic start, San Franciscans and other visitors from the north slip down Skyline Boulevard from Crystal Springs Reservoir to Saratoga Gap, then down State 9 into Saratoga.

The Skyline does what its name suggests. It stays on top of the immediate world, the backbone of the Santa Cruz Mountains. A good, lightly-trafficked, two-lane road, it provides a whole series of sweeping views east over San Francisco Bay and the Santa Clara Valley. On the other side the sweeping views are fewer but include a few distant seascapes. Sometimes the hills are open and grassy, sometimes tightly furred with conifer woods.

State 9 down into Saratoga follows a snaking creek through a vegetative cover that plainly reveals increasing warmth with decreasing elevation.

For the hurried, U.S. 101 (the Bayshore Freeway) steams straight and fast from San Francisco into San Jose. Interstate 280 connects the same two cities and is almost as fast, in spite of its scenic route through coast hill country. On the east side of the bay, State 17 (Nimitz Freeway) is a counterpart to U.S. 101.

State 17 curves west across the foot of the bay, crosses U.S. 101 and Interstate 280 in quick succession, and then continues through Los Gatos all the way to the shore at Santa Cruz. State 85 connects U.S. 101 and Interstate 280 a few miles north at Mountain View. These four freeways form a tidy grid that puts all of the district wineries within easy reach of one another. (See the map on page 63.)

Anybody approaching from the south has no choice but U.S. 101 unless he is really after a slow way. The confirmed shunpike can cruise County Route G8 from Gilroy through the hills to Blossom Hill Road.

The Monte Sereno Road is a quick way between Saratoga and Los Gatos, as well as an invitingly scenic one. A number of other local roads poke up into the hill country west of these two towns. Bear Creek Road and Pierce Road have some practical values as well as scenic ones because they lead from major routes to wineries.

SOUTH SANTA CLARA

The Santa Clara Valley cuts a straight swath south from San Jose to the Santa Clara-San Benito County line a few miles south of Gilroy. U.S. 101, part original, part new freeway, gives a fair impression of what the country-side is like. For wine buffs, though, the focal points require some delving into local nooks and crannies.

West of U.S. 101, the district called Hecker Pass is made of vine-filled bottomlands, grassy hills, oak knolls, cactus farms, wandering creeks and reservoirs, the beginnings of conifer forests just below the namesake pass, and a nest of small wineries. The names, mostly Roman, are legion. (The roster starts with Bertero, ends with Scagliotti.) Some of the wineries have tasting rooms. All sell wine at the door for modest prices. None is big enough to require a tour.

Still more wineries flank U.S. 101 on its east side from Morgan Hill down to Gilroy.

Gilroy, the major center, has revitalized its downtown district since being bypassed by the new stretch of freeway U.S. 101. What used to be a tedious stretch of stop-lighted highway now has become a stylish shopping street. The landmark building remains unchanged. It is the old city hall, built a year before the great earthquake of 1906. Having survived the quake, the structure has provided continuous wonderment to students of architecture ever since.

In season, a heavy, sweet aroma of drying fruit hangs in the still air, even in the middle of town. This is prune and apricot as much as grape country, and the dehydrators perfume the district for week after warm summer week.

Hecker Pass Wineries

The several small wineries of the Hecker Pass district resemble one another far more closely than do the collected cellars of any other district in the state. Buildings, equipment, and wine lists all share their basic qualities, leaving only details to separate each from the next. Hardly anywhere can visitors learn better how much the human element counts in winemaking because the external similarities of these places camouflage their strong individual characters.

What is more, the lesson can be learned in a small space. Half a dozen wineries cluster as tightly as grapes along the stem of State 152, the Hecker Pass Highway, west of Gilroy. Yet another cellar hides away on County Route G8 not far off the state road. The list is alphabetical.

Bertero Winery, set well back from the highway behind a stucco house, a wood-frame visitor center, and a substantial block of vines, dates back almost as far as wineries date in Gilroy.

Alfonso Bertero opened the doors in 1917. The second and third generations carry the name forward in

HECKER PASS *vineyards are set in rolling coastal hills typical of California around San Francisco Bay.*

somewhat enlarged premises. Bertero, the father, built his winery of redwood, having dug a 4-foot-deep trench in the middle as an insulating device for the redwood tanks. (It is almost a sure thing that a winery with such a device was designed and built by an Italian.) His building has been augmented by a concrete block addition.

The pavilionlike tasting room, handsomely set in the vineyards, is the starting point for visitors. From it, the Berteros launch tours of the vineyard and winery proper, throwing in asides on an enormous oak tree and the whereabouts of marker stakes from the original Spanish land grant, all of which are well to the rear of the property from the tasting room.

The wine list, all of it available for tasting, spreads more widely than most in the area: Barbera, Cabernet Sauvignon, Grignolino, Pinot Noir, and Zinfandel are the reds. A couple of whites and a rosé round out the table wine roster. There are also sparkling wines, Vermouth, Dry Sherry, Cream Sherry, and Tawny Port.

Conrotto announces the winery with a standard rural mailbox — no more, no less. The modesty is too much. This is a good-size establishment of its kind.

The wines — red, white, and rosé — go mostly to the restaurant trade, but the proprietor will sell them on the premises in lots of a case or more, mainly in jugs.

There is no tasting. Neither is there a tour of the premises, which run for a surprising distance beyond the front wall.

Fortino Winery is a relatively new name on a relatively old place.

Veteran visitors to the Hecker Pass region will remember the cream-colored stucco building as the Cassa Brothers' plant. The Ernest Fortino family bought the winery and vineyards from the last survivor of the founding family in 1970 and set about revamping both the property and the list of wines.

By and large, the Cassas had stayed with the traditional red, white, and rosé of the district. The Fortinos, though, lean toward varietal table wines, including Cabernet Sauvignon and Petit Syrah. (They spell it the ancient Mediterranean way, with the "y.") These and their other wines are on hand in a small tasting room located approximately amidships.

The tour of a well-ordered cellar full of upright redwood tanks is almost sure to be led by a Fortino. And this is an informative winery to visit in vintage season. The old basket press and other working parts are out in full view to demonstrate the traditional way to make wine.

Hecker Pass Winery directly adjoins the Fortino Winery; it is owned by a different family of Fortinos. Mario and Frances Fortino launched their small cellar in 1972 but did not open it to tour until their first wines were ready for tasting in 1974.

Mario Fortino came to the United States from Italy in 1959 and worked for other cellars in the Santa Clara region — full-time until he founded his own winery, part-time until the tasting room was well established. Some outgrowths of his earlier employment show up in the working winery. The basket presses and redwood fermenting tanks at the rear are typical of old-line Gilroy, but, inside, Fortino has a temperature-controlled stainless steel tank for fermenting his white wine. Pumps and other equipment also suggest technical skills. For the most part, the aging cellar is small oak.

The wines, most of them labeled as "Estate Bottled" and vintage dated, including Carignane, Cabernet Sauvignon, Petite Sirah, and Zinfandel. Chablis is the white representative.

Kirigin Cellars was formerly known as Bonesio Winery. Nikola Kirigin Chargin purchased the picturesque property in 1976 and renamed it for the Kirigin family, who were winegrowers for five generations on the Adriatic Coast of Croatia.

Both Uvas wines and estate-bottled Kirigin Cellars wines, including Cabernet Sauvignon, Pinot Noir, Malvasia Bianca, and Zinfandel, are available in the tasting room. The winery also sells a few fruit, apéritif, and specialty wines.

The historic homestead, built in 1827, was renovated in 1976. (Originally the mansion of Henry Miller, a local cattle baron, the house was moved from high up Mt. Madonna into the Uvas Valley to shelter the Bonesio family.)

The front lawn has a shaded picnic area for up to 30 visitors.

SOUTH SANTA CLARA

BERTERO. S side S.R. 152, 4 mi. W of Bus. 101. (3920 Hecker Pass Hwy., Gilroy 95020. Tel [408] 842-3032) Daily, 9-6 summer, 9-5 winter. IT/Ta

FORTINO. N side of S.R. 152, 5¼ mi. W of Bus. 101. (4525 Hecker Pass Hwy., Gilroy 95020. Tel [408] 842-3305) Daily, 9-6. GT/Ta

EMILIO GUGLIELMO. From Bus. 101 in Morgan Hill, E 1½ mi. on Main Ave. (1480 E. Main Ave., Morgan Hill 95037. Tel [408] 779-3064) Daily, 8-5. Ta

HECKER PASS. N side of S.R. 152, 5½ mi. W of Bus. 101. (4605 Hecker Pass Hwy., Gilroy 95020. Tel [408] 842-8755) Daily, 8-6. GT/Ta

KIRIGIN CELLARS. From Bus. 101, W 5 mi. on S.R. 152, N 2½ mi. on County G8. Winery on E side of rd. (11550 Watsonville Rd., Gilroy 95020. Tel [408] 847-8827) Picnic; groups must reserve. Daily, 9-6.

THOMAS KRUSE. S side S.R. 152, 5 mi. W of Bus. 101. (4390 Hecker Pass Hwy., Gilroy 95020. Tel [408] 842-7016) Picnic. F-Su, or by appt., 12-6. IT/Ta

LIVE OAKS. N side S.R. 152, 4 mi. W of Bus. 101. (3875 Hecker Pass Hwy., Gilroy 95020. Tel [408] 842-2401) Daily, 8-5. Ta

LOS ALTOS. E. side U.S. 101, 3 mi. S of Gilroy. (PO Box 247, Gilroy 95020. Tel [408] 842-5649) Daily, summer 9-8, winter 9-6. Ta

PEDRIZZETTI. Tasting room: N limit of Morgan Hill, E side of Bus. 101. Winery: From Bus. 101 in Morgan Hill, E on Dunne Ave. East to Murphy, S to San Pedro Ave., then E. (Rt. 2, Box 166, Morgan Hill 95037. Tel [408] 779-7389) M-Sa, 8-6. Tours by appt.

SAN MARTIN. E. side Bus. 101, 2 mi. S of Morgan Hill; 5 mi. N of Gilroy. (PO Box 53, San Martin 95046. Tel [408] 683-2672) Daily, 9-7:30 summer, 9-6 winter. Ta

WINERIES OUTSIDE OF MAP AREA

ALMADEN (tasting rooms, San Benito County). San Juan Bautista: SE corner of town plaza. Daily, 10-4. Pachecho Pass: at jct. of S.R. 152 and 156. Daily, 10-4:30.

ENZ VINEYARDS. (1781 Limekiln Rd., Hollister 95023. [408] 673-3956) Visits by appt.

KEY: GT (guided tour); IT (informal tour); Ta (tasting).

Thomas Kruse Winery, right across Hecker Pass Highway from the end of County Route G8, departs in a couple of ways from the general habits of the district.

For one thing, the name Kruse sticks out just a little bit in this quintessentially Italian roster of wineries. For another, its proprietor ferments and ages all of his wines in small oak barrels rather than in upright redwood tanks. For still a third, Kruse elects to make wines of types and styles not common to Gilroy. His wine list in spring, 1975, included such individual items as a white sparkling wine made from Zinfandel grapes, a bone-dry rosé from Grignolino, and a 15 percent alcohol red called Late-Harvest Carignane.

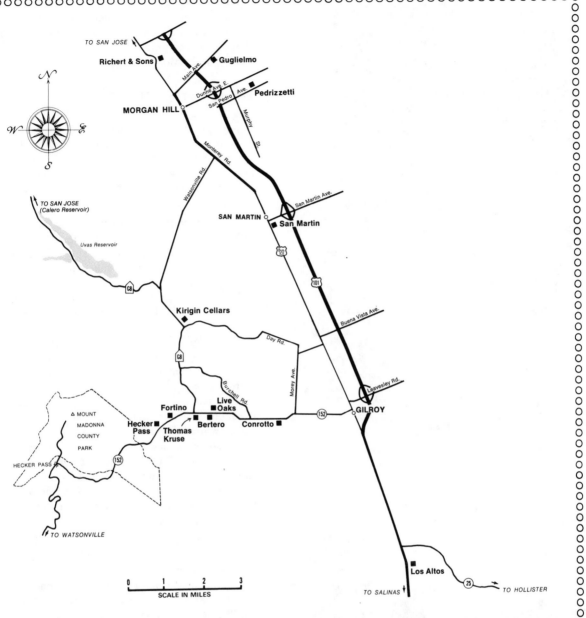

The map shows wineries in the Morgan Hill, San Martin, and Gilroy areas of the Central Coast. Labeled locations include: Richert & Sons, Guglielmo, Pedrizzetti, Morgan Hill, San Martin, Kirigin Cellars, Fortino, Live Oaks, Bertero, Thomas Kruse, Hecker Pass, Conrotto, Gilroy, Los Altos. Roads include Main Ave., Dunne Ave. E., San Pedro Ave., Murphy St., Monterey Rd., Watsonville Rd., San Martin Ave., Day Rd., Buena Vista Ave., Morey Ave., Burchell Rd., Leavesley Rd., and routes 101, G8, 152, and 25. Mount Madonna County Park and Uvas Reservoir are shown. Directions: TO SAN JOSE, TO SAN JOSE (Calero Reservoir), TO WATSONVILLE, TO SALINAS, TO HOLLISTER.

SCALE IN MILES 0 1 2 3

Kruse acquired the property in 1971. The physical premises are undergoing a continuous rehabilitation, having survived without much repair since 1910. Visitors are welcome to browse over the construction as well as the winemaking apparatus. The informal atmosphere is unfailingly cheerful.

Live Oaks Winery advertises itself best of the several along the highway. A platoon of signs on the north side of the road invites visitors to turn alongside an eclectic lot of frame buildings until the drive dips downhill and ends alongside a white-painted, board-and-batten winery.

In all its casual and good-humored aspects, this winery typifies what the Hecker Pass district is: a source of modestly priced, unpretentious, everyday wine made in and offered from an appropriate kind of winery.

Live Oaks' tasting room has paneled wall on one side, stainless steel bottling tanks on the other, stuffed birds and animal heads wherever space permits, and case goods stacked as owner Peter Scagliotti's need requires. Tours of the fermenting area go on during the fall vintage.

The Live Oaks label, which has been around since 1912, appears on red, white, and rosé — two wines of each type. Scagliotti offers a line in fifths and, for even less cost, a line in half-gallon and gallon jugs.

REPEAT CUSTOMERS *carry cases of empty bottles to Live Oaks Winery, to be replaced with full ones.*

PROPRIETORS WELCOME *visitors to friendly tasting room of tiny, traditional Hecker Pass Winery.*

Miscellaneous Wineries. New names are cropping up here as in nearly all other California wine districts. In addition to Kirigin Cellars (the new name on the old Bonesio property), a winery named Sycamore Creek is located in the Morgan Hill area.

Wineries Near U.S. 101

In addition to the tight cluster of wineries in the Hecker Pass district, southern Santa Clara County has another, looser bunch strung out along U.S. 101 from Morgan Hill down to Gilroy. Though fewer in number than their Hecker Pass neighbors, these wineries are more diverse in size and character.

Emilio Guglielmo Winery, a mile east of U.S. 101 at Morgan Hill, has several unexpected aspects.

Largely anonymous after a long career in the bulk wine trade, the winery is much larger than its wines' rare appearances in stores might indicate. In addition to being sizable, the operation is up-to-the-minute technologically. (The long row of stainless steel fermentors at the rear, for example, is of an unusual type developed in Australia. The floors — instead of sloping all in one direction — are conical, so that grape solids can be emptied automatically through a door right at the bottom.)

The main aging cellar is full of wooden cooperage, a tradition as old as stainless steel is new.

The winery does not offer tours, only tasting in a small room hidden behind a stucco house. There, old-line customers know to look for jugs of generic wines under the Emile's label. A more recent development is a line of varietals, many vintage dated, under the Mt. Madonna label. (The name comes from the tall, conical peak that looms up on the west horizon.)

Los Altos Winery, a bit more than 2 miles south of Gilroy on U.S. 101, has only a tasting room open to visitors. The range of wines here is wide. The list of varietals extends to Green Hungarian among the whites and Barbera among reds, along with all of the more familiar names. Appetizer and dessert wines are similarly numerous. Some are labeled as Los Altos, some as Rappazzini Brothers. (The brothers are the proprietors.)

In 1972 they opened a second tasting room under the name Stagecoach Cellars. This outlet is on U.S. 101 several miles south of the original at Aromas, across the line into Monterey County.

Pedrizzetti Winery maintains its public face in a building of several uses on business U.S. 101, just at the northern outskirts of Morgan Hill.

There the Pedrizzetti tasting room shares a roadside stucco building with an art gallery and small restaurant.

The emphasis in recent years has changed from country-style mid-varietals and generic wines to a line of such varietals as Johannisberg Riesling, Chardonnay, Petite Sirah, and Cabernet Sauvignon.

The producing winery, just about midway between

the new freeway (U.S. 101) and the east hills, houses an amazing mixture of old and new equipment. The press, for example, is a Willmes from Germany. It feeds both concrete and stainless steel fermentors. So goes the story from start to finish, the total effect somehow managing to be orderly.

On San Pedro Avenue, the low, rambling building is not open for casual visits. Still, a drive past reveals most of what there is to know, and it can be incorporated into an excursion to Anderson Lake County Park.

San Martin Vineyards does not open its producing winery to visitors. The founding Filice family felt that the archaically constructed building offered too difficult a maze to strangers. The more recent corporate ownership, Southdown, has been renovating the old property so continuously that it has retained the old policy.

Yet the firm does operate tasting rooms in numbers. The principal one adjoins the producing winery at San Martin, on Business U.S. 101. (Others are several miles south of Gilroy on U.S. 101 and in the cities of San Jose, Morgan Hill, and Monterey.)

The long, low main building at the winery has a tasting area at either end. The south station takes care of overflow crowds or visitors who wish to sample one or two specific wines as a buying guide. The larger area at the north wall offers sequences of wines for informal groups, with commentary on each taste from the host. These exercises — frequent, brief, and never formidable — show wine in the wide diversity of its flavors. A tasting usually includes dry table wines from a full roster of varietals, slightly sweet table wines from San Martin's "Hostess" line, and some flavored wines from among the appetizer and dessert bottles.

ooooooooooooooo

Falling between Santa Clara and Monterey counties are Almaden's large San Benito County holdings and the much smaller ones of Enz Vineyards.

Almaden has its red wine winery at La Cienega. Vast blocks of vines grow here and in the Salinas Valley. This winery has no visitor facilities, but the firm welcomes visitors at a tasting room on the plaza in San Juan Bautista.

Enz Vineyards near Hollister is the property of Robert and Susan Enz. Bonded in 1973, its original vineyards date to 1895. Estate-bottled wines, Pinot St. George, Zinfandel (red and rosé), and the rarely bottled Golden Chasselas (a cousin of the Swiss Fendant), are on sale at the winery.

Other Than Wineries

Several pleasing and temptingly diverse parks line the hills on either side of the southern Santa Clara Valley.

Dry and parched as the east hills appear from U.S. 101, they hide a string of reservoirs, each developed for recreation.

The most highly developed of the lot is Anderson Lake County Park, in the first range of hills east of Morgan

HOST POURS sample for a student in San Martin winery's 20-minute course for wine tasters.

EL TOROS CHARGE across the smooth surface of Uvas Reservoir at four in the afternoon. Uvas is one of several boatable lakes tucked into the hills of south Santa Clara County near Gilroy.

Hill. Cochran Road (the temporary connector between old U.S. 101 and the new freeway U.S. 101) goes directly to the main area. Although primarily developed for boaters, the shore has a large picnic area. At the southern tip of the same lake is a second picnic area, this one reached on East Dunne Avenue.

Henry W. Coe State Park lies directly east of Anderson Lake on an extension of East Dunne Avenue. The distance from downtown Morgan Hill is 14 miles.

A one-time working ranch, the headquarters of Coe are in the old ranch buildings at an elevation of 2,600 feet. Both these and the park's rolling, grassy hills attract watercolorists by the score, especially in late April and May when the wildflowers bloom. There are some picnic sites and a few campsites. Expect a day-use fee.

Farther south, Coyote Lake County Park offers a third choice. Again, a reservoir is the prime attraction, with shoreside picnicking as a most welcome supplement to the charms of the place. Access is from Gilroy on Leavesley Road.

Over in the west hills, Mt. Madonna County Park has its main entrance at the summit of the Hecker Pass. Like Henry W. Coe State Park, this area has been built out of a one-time working ranch. Cattleman Henry Miller owned it and left some formal gardens to posterity. Otherwise, the park has a herd of albino deer as a special attraction. Roads meander through the oak-forested hills at the upper elevations.

At the foot of the hills, next to a creek and pond, are picnic sites in the shade of oak and other trees. The entrance is from State 152. There is a day-use fee for this park, too.

County Route G8 threads its way through the west hills, touching three reservoirs as it goes. The most southerly is Uvas. Then comes Chesbro. Calero is the northernmost, a fair distance north of Morgan Hill. Reachable from U.S. 101 on Bailey Avenue as well as by G8, Chesbro is the most thoroughly developed of the three reservoirs for picnickers.

Plotting a Route

U.S. 101 brings traffic into southern Santa Clara County from both north and south. State 152, called the Hecker Pass Highway west of U.S. 101 and the Pachecho Pass Highway east of it, handles the cross traffic.

U.S. 101 is principally a divided freeway now, except for one stretch between Morgan Hill and the southern fringe of San Jose and another one just south of the Santa Clara County line. The road keeps to the flat but also runs close enough to the hills to remain more pleasant than many freeways.

The Pacheco Pass Highway, winding and scenic, carries a great amount of truck traffic in and out of the Central Valley and also serves as a link in the much-traveled road to Yosemite National Park. It is hardly ever lonely. The Hecker Pass segment of the road does not climb so high nor serve so many uses. Connecting Gilroy and Watsonville, it is popular enough, mainly for the views from the summit.

Not many local roads supplement the major highways.

Old U.S. 101, now known as Business U.S. 101, runs through the business districts of Gilroy and Morgan Hill.

County Route G8 is a narrow and winding way between Gilroy and San Jose and also the means of getting to several reservoirs and picnic parks.

Where G8 forks left toward the hills, another road eases right and back toward Morgan Hill. It stays with farms and houses, including one zinnia patch and one tiny commercial mushroom farm.

MIST IRRIGATION is a clever enough imitation of rain to fool young San Martin vines in Monterey County.

 ## MONTEREY COUNTY

In the mid-1970s, Monterey County hovered on the brink of becoming a major tourable wine district. If all the plans then afoot go forward, wine buffs can visit a great deal of vinous Monterey before the decade comes to an end.

The development can only astonish anyone schooled in the slow cadences of traditional wine growing.

In the early 1960s, Monterey County had approximately 100 acres of vineyard in all its length and breadth. The 1974 total exceeded an impressive 37,000 acres.

The roster of owners of these vineyards includes many familiar names, several new ones, and, of course, the chap who pioneered most of that original 100 acres.

The pioneer is Chalone Vineyards. The familiar names include Almaden, Paul Masson, Mirassou Vineyards, San Martin, and Wente Bros. The newcomers range from the awesomely large and complicated The Monterey Vineyard through the small Greenfield Vineyards to the tiny Durney Vineyards.

All of these wineries (along with a good many vineyard owners who do not have wineries) belong to an association that has, as one goal, the early development of wine-oriented tourism in its district. This area extends through much of the length of the Salinas Valley from Gonzales down to King City. Most of the old-name companies with producing wineries in other districts are committed to opening tasting rooms in the region. These, coupled with local producing wineries, will give the valley enough points of interest to require 2 or 3 days of diligent study on the part of serious students.

In the meantime, enough local wineries open their doors to give at least 1 day of instructive rounds.

The Wineries

Two wineries with their producing facilities in the Salinas Valley of Monterey County presently welcome visitors. They are the largest and smallest of the purely local firms — and also the oldest and one of the newest.

Chalone Vineyard is the tiny pioneer. The oldest vines, on a gentle slope just below a dramatic rock outcropping of the Pinnacles National Monument, were planted in 1919 by a man named Bill Silvear, who put them on the site of an even older vineyard.

MATURE VINEYARDS of Chalone bask in late sun below craggy basalt of Pinnacles National Monument.

INSIDE A CELLAR, a mixture of stainless steel, redwood, and oak reflects many possibilities for aging wine.

MONTEREY VINEYARDS winery draws its architectural flavor from a miscellany of early California sources.

After Silvear died in 1957, the vines endured ups and downs until 1965, when the present owners bought the property. Interim owners had built a small winery but had made very little wine before suspending operations.

Now Chalone goes forward, under the stewardship of Dick Graff, as both vineyard and winery, producing Chardonnay, Pinot Blanc, Chenin Blanc, Pinot Noir, and California Champagne. Chalone ferments and ages its wines in small barrels of Limousin oak and otherwise is a hand-labor sort of winery. It must be. There is no electricity.

Though there is no tasting, the owners will conduct thorough tours by appointment. Appointments must be made by mail. Chalone is 14 miles beyond the end of the nearest telephone wire. Directions come with appointment.

Monterey Peninsula (bonded in 1974) is the winery of dentists Deryck Nuckton and Roy Thomas (winemaker), who turned a hobby into a commercial venture.

They own no vineyards, choosing instead to buy grapes from selected corners of northern California.

The Monterey Peninsula label covers favored varietal bottlings and Monterey Cellars is used for some varietals, generics, and fruit wines. Most can be explored and discussed in the tasting room.

The winery is a local landmark; its stone, Spanish-tiled buildings once housed the Cadematore restaurant. (A branch tasting room is in Carmel.)

The Monterey Vineyard winery buildings loom up alongside U.S. 101 on the south side of Gonzales, a dramatic set of structures in a region that has very few large buildings.

The impression fits. This is a dramatic enterprise. All told, the winery is designed to crush the grapes from 9,600 acres of vineyards scattered through the region in 28 separate parcels. One building has been designed to make red wines. A second, still to be constructed as of 1977, is to make all the whites.

Architecturally, the style is called "early California" by the proprietors — which is to say an amalgamation of mission, adobe, and Spanish colonial influences. Arches and towers are the distinguishing marks, along with tile roofs.

Visitors can work their way through the whole complex on a carefully engineered route that takes them past the crushers and presses, into the fermenting hall, and through aging cellars full of large and small cooperage.

Close attention to the gear will show any number of unusual details. One such is a system of closed conveyors for moving pomace and lees (solid residues) out of the fermentors and to the presses or filters. Another is a system of palletized barrels in the small wood aging cellar, the purpose in this case being to hasten the jobs of emptying and cleaning the barrels when the wine in them goes to bottle.

Most of these details were designed by the winemaker-president, Dr. Richard Peterson. (To make the winery still more of a family affair, his artist-wife, Diane, designed the tall stained-glass windows in the walls of the main building.)

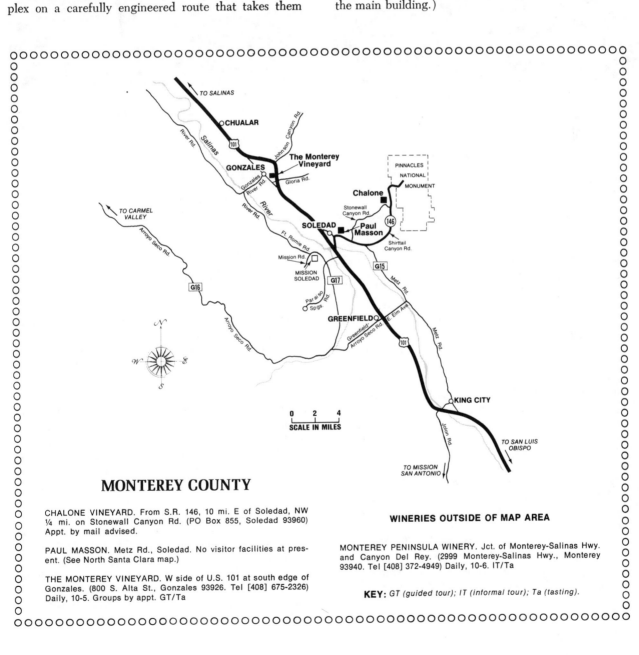

MONTEREY COUNTY

CHALONE VINEYARD. From S.R. 146, 10 mi. E of Soledad, NW ¼ mi. on Stonewall Canyon Rd. (PO Box 855, Soledad 93960) Appt. by mail advised.

PAUL MASSON. Metz Rd., Soledad. No visitor facilities at present. (See North Santa Clara map.)

THE MONTEREY VINEYARD. W side of U.S. 101 at south edge of Gonzales. (800 S. Alta St., Gonzales 93926. Tel [408] 675-2326) Daily, 10-5. Groups by appt. GT/Ta

WINERIES OUTSIDE OF MAP AREA

MONTEREY PENINSULA WINERY. Jct. of Monterey-Salinas Hwy. and Canyon Del Rey. (2999 Monterey-Salinas Hwy., Monterey 93940. Tel [408] 372-4949) Daily, 10-6. IT/Ta

KEY: GT (guided tour); IT (informal tour); Ta (tasting).

PAUL MASSON Soledad winery sits among rolling waves of vines in the southeast quarter of Soledad town.

MIRASSOU VINES near Soledad are in rolling hills typical of the west side of the Salinas Valley.

In the tasting room, most of the wines are varietals, including Chardonnay, Chenin Blanc, Grüner Sylvaner, Johannisberg Riesling, and Sauvignon Blanc among whites, and Gamay and Zinfandel among reds. (Cabernet Sauvignon and Pinot Noir will join the list as they mature. The Monterey Vineyard's first crush was 1974.)

There are also wines named after the individual vineyards in which their grapes grew. The first one released, a white, is called Del Mar Ranch.

Miscellaneous Wineries. Paul Masson and Durney presently have wineries in the region. Greenfield Vineyard (Turgeon & Lohr Winery, see page 67), Mirassou Vineyard, and San Martin all have their producing wineries elsewhere.

The Masson facility, on Metz Road (State 146) at the southeast corner of Soledad, is another giant on the same scale as The Monterey Vineyard. It was built without visitors in mind, though, and likely will never be able to accommodate visitors because the complex working parts are crowded into the buildings. Paul Masson welcomes visitors at its Saratoga facility (see page 62).

Durney Vineyard is not in the Salinas River watershed but rather in that of the Carmel River. The proprietor had not opened his winery and vineyard to the public when the first wines went to market in 1975.

Mirassou Vineyard has two ranches in Monterey County (one west of Soledad, the other north and east of it) and a producing winery in the old Evergreen district near San Jose. The family firm welcomes visitors at the winery (see page 64).

Finally, San Martin has its principal vineyard among the huge expanses of vines on Jolon Road west of King City. The company has its producing winery at San Martin, near Morgan Hill. Its main tasting room is there. Others are at Bloomfield, on U.S. 101 south of Gilroy, and on Fisherman's Wharf at Monterey city.

Other Than Wineries

In addition to its vineyards and wineries, the Salinas Valley has an engaging admixture of the works of God — and of the works of man on behalf of that God.

The pure article is Pinnacles National Monument, an imposing array of columnar basalt and lava caves left over from one of the more explosively formative moments of the local landscape. The monument is high in the hills that form the east side of the valley.

Much the greater development — including the visitor center and campgrounds — is on the east side of the monument, reached from Hollister along State 25. No road crosses the monument from west to east, but a fair sampler of the lava caves and some lunar-looking terrain crops up at the end of State 146, which departs from downtown Soledad and arrives some 40 minutes later in the monument.

Incidentally, the fogs and breezes that cool the valley floor do not penetrate to the Pinnacles, which, though temperate in spring and fall, are downright hot in summer.

Two of California's 21 Franciscan missions are in the vineyarded reaches of the Salinas Valley. They are Soledad and San Antonio. A third, San Miguel, is no great distance to the south along U.S. 101.

Soledad Mission — Mission Nuestra Señora de la Soledad, to give it its full name — has only one mostly melted adobe wall surviving from the original complex. (A chapel of newer style flanks it.) In its forlorn way, the old wall tells the history of the region. Soledad was essentially a desolate, lonely failure among the missions. The primary lack was available water. The Franciscans had no idea that the Salinas River was so full of water because none showed on top. One of the many crops they could not grow was grapes.

Nowadays, the new wave of vineyardists does a joyous victory dance right on the spot. Each September brings a mission festival and treading of the grapes on the grounds. Fair maidens compete to see which among them has the most efficient feet for crushing grapes. The results of their labors are fermented by Mirassou Vineyards and sold at auction during the following year's festival. Proceeds go to a restoration fund for the mission.

The mission stands west of U.S. 101 on Paraiso Springs and Fort Romie roads.

A far truer look at how life went in the mission days can be had at Mission San Antonio de Padua, located in a high valley west of the main Salinas River Valley, approximately level with King City. Jolon Road leads to it from U.S. 101.

Most completely and most accurately restored of all the Franciscan missions along the El Camino Real, San Antonio has the priceless further advantage of a location with even fewer inhabitants now than it had at the height of the mission era. In short, the broad, grassy plain in front of the mission and the oak-covered slopes behind it look much as they did between 1780 and 1830.

Within, the building has restorations or replicas of a great deal of working mission gear. Included is the old wine cellar, a structure guaranteed to gladden the hearts of all who drink wine from newer, more manageable fermentors and aging cellars.

Picnickers in search of a table in the Salinas Valley have only a handful of choices. A few flank the chapel grounds at Mission Soledad. The other choice is a sizable municipal park at King City, on the east side of U.S. 101 midway between the two freeway exits leading into town.

Plotting a Route

For visitors from either north or south, U.S. 101 is the obvious means for getting into the Salinas Valley. It also is a quick means for getting from one town to the next — but only when haste matters more than a good smell of the flowers.

A fair proportion of visitors may come from the Monterey Peninsula. For them, State 68 from Monterey to Salinas, then U.S. 101 south to the vineyard region, is the efficient route. A pleasing variation is State 68 as far as its intersection with River Road, then River Road south along the edge of the valley to Greenfield or beyond. River Road, a two-laner with some slow stretches,

MISSION SOLEDAD grounds provide restful interlude for winery and vineyard visitors to Monterey County.

MISSION SAN ANTONIO preserves as well as any the tranquil flavor of the original mission days.

is shorter enough in miles to compensate for fewer miles per hour. In addition, the farm scenery and the hills compose themselves into finer scenes than the remote ones visible from freeway U.S. 101.

The slowest of all routes between the coast and the valley is Carmel Valley Road-Arroyo Seco Road, which wanders erratically through the broad expanse of high hills separating sea from vines, finally bringing one to Greenfield after a long, dry, but scenically rewarding drive.

For tourists coming from the San Joaquin Valley, State 152 (the Pacheco Pass Highway) to San Juan Bautista, then U.S. 101 south is virtually the lone choice.

Within the region, except for State 146 curling up into dramatic hill country on the east side of the valley, most of the pleasing local roads crisscross the terrain west of U.S. 101, sometimes on the flat but frequently just up on the shoulders of the hills. Here is the place for photographers to go hunting for dramatic scenes of rolling vineyard.

Greenfield-Arroyo Seco Road at Greenfield, Paraiso Springs Road at Soledad, and Gonzales River Road at Gonzales are the principal access roads to all the others in the northern half of the district. Toward King City, Jolon Road leads to some awesome vineyard vistas.

 ## SANTA CRUZ COUNTY

Santa Cruz County has a wide circle of admirers for a number of reasons. One is Big Basins Redwoods State Park in its mountainous east side. Another is the shore of Monterey Bay, dotted with several state parks and crowned by the resort town of Santa Cruz.

The county also has wineries, but just one is open for casual visits.

Bargetto Winery is located in the town of Soquel, just inland from the main business intersection. It is housed in a trimly painted red barn that looks just as solid as it is.

The second generation of Bargettos owns it now. John Bargetto and a brother founded it in 1933, and John had a firm hand in the business until his death in 1964. His son Lawrence continues the operation.

There are tours of the premises, starting at the crusher out front and ending at the tasting room on the west end of the building.

In it, Bargetto offers a substantial number of varietal (Pinot Noir, Zinfandel, Pinot Blanc, Muscato Amabile) and generic table wines, some fairly ancient dessert wines, and Vermouths. They have a second label of generic table and dessert wines.

In addition to being handy to the resort town of Santa Cruz, Soquel is only a moment's detour off State 1. Beach-bound picnickers and anybody en route to Monterey can dip into town with ease.

Miscellaneous Wineries. In and around the Santa Cruz Mountains small wineries come and go. Founded in the 1970s are Roudon-Smith six miles north of Santa Cruz on Mt. View Road, Two Friends at the former Hallcrest Winery near Felton, and P & M Staiger near Boulder Creek. All of these require specific appointments to visit.

 ## SAN LUIS OBISPO– SANTA BARBARA

In recent history, San Luis Obispo County has had only a tiny, single-minded sort of wine community. Three small wineries have long taken the crop from some 400 acres of vines, nearly all Zinfandels, and made it into wine to be sold locally.

The old district, west of Templeton, dates back to the 1850s, without any great change anywhere along the line.

After 100 years the revolution is coming. The county now boasts 4,100 acres of vineyards and the old list of three wineries is beginning to grow.

Farther south, in Santa Barbara County, 6,000 acres of vines have been planted since 1971 and the Firestone family operates a pioneering winery.

Wineries in the two counties appear alphabetically.

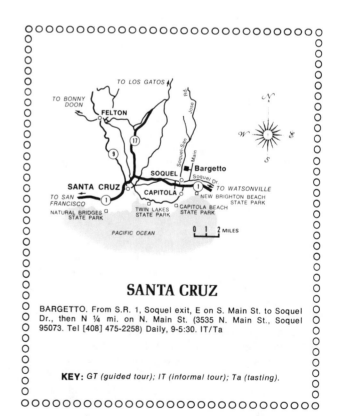

SANTA CRUZ

BARGETTO. From S.R. 1, Soquel exit, E on S. Main St. to Soquel Dr., then N ¼ mi. on N. Main St. (3535 N. Main St., Soquel 95073. Tel [408] 475-2258) Daily, 9-5:30. IT/Ta

KEY: *GT (guided tour); IT (informal tour); Ta (tasting).*

The Firestone Vineyard planted 300 acres of vines in 1972 surrounding the winery site in the Santa Ynez Valley. The first crush took place in 1975 with the showcase winery still under construction.

The first wine, Rosé of Cabernet Sauvignon, was released in 1976; to follow are Johannisberg Riesling, Gewürztraminer, Chardonnay, Cabernet Sauvignon, and Pinot Noir.

The production goal is 75,000 cases of estate wines.

Tours and tasting are by appointment, but there are retail sales at the winery.

Hoffman Mountain Ranch is located 7 miles southwest of Paso Robles in the cool, sometimes foggy foothills of the Santa Lucia Mountain Range.

Founder-owner Dr. Stanley Hoffman and sons David and Michael knew about the difficult terrain and the gravelly soil when they planted the vineyard in 1962, but they felt the climate was right.

The first wines were made in 1972 before there was a winery building. Completed in fall, 1975, the building is a well-designed, two-level wood structure of handsome proportions filled with the latest equipment.

The wines include Franken Riesling, Chenin Blanc, Pinot Noir, Cabernet Sauvignon, and Zinfandel. They can be sampled and purchased at the winery's tasting room near the Black Oak restaurant in Paso Robles. Winery visits are by appointment.

Pesenti Winery dates only from 1934, when Frank Pesenti founded the company. He has since taken on two partners (son Victor Pesenti and Aldo Nerelli) and completed the main winery building (in 1947).

In the early days, San Joaquin Valley shepherds bought much of the wine to take away in their own jugs, or, just as likely, in Basque *botas*. Nowadays, it is all bottled and available for tasting in a pleasantly appointed room. The reds are all home-grown from a vineyard that has recently had Cabernet Sauvignon, Grenache, and Carignane grapes added to the original planting of Zinfandel.

Rotta Winery, one mailbox away from Pesenti, has a longer history. It was founded in 1856 by Adolph Siot, who planted the first Zinfandels in the district. The Swiss family Rotta acquired the property from its original holder in 1907. The winery has been going at a steady pace since then. It is housed in a white, barnlike structure. Visitors can amble through with a guide, who will point out which parts go back to founder Siot, and then end up with a practical tasting of the Zinfandel and other wines.

York Mountain Winery is several miles to the west of its companion cellars in the region and, because of its lofty elevation in the Coast Ranges, is subject to an added 20 inches of rain each year. York, like Rotta, is old in this district. A Texan, Jacob R. Grandstaff, launched the winery in 1875 to absorb an excess of grapes from

SAN LUIS OBISPO

HOFFMAN MOUNTAIN RANCH. Tasting room in Paso Robles at corner of U.S. 101 and Hwy. 46 by way of 24th St. exit. (Adelaida Rd., Star Rt., Paso Robles 93446. Tel [805] 238-4945) Tasting room open M-F, 11-7; Sa, Su, holidays, 9-7. Winery tours by appt. only.

PESENTI. From U.S. 101, Vineyard Dr. exit, W 2½ mi. on Vineyard Dr. (Rt. 1, Box 169, Templeton 93465. Tel [805] 434-1030) M-Sa, 8-6; Su, 10-6. Ta

ROTTA. From U.S. 101, Vineyard Dr. exit, W 3 mi. on Vineyard Dr. (Rt. 1, Box 168, Templeton 93465. Tel [805] 434-1389) Daily, 8-5. GT/Ta

YORK MOUNTAIN. From U.S. 101, W 9 mi. on S.R. 46, then N on York Mtn. Rd. Or: E from S.R. 1, 12 mi. to York Mtn. Rd. (Rt. 1, Box 191, Templeton 93465. Tel [805] 238-3925) Daily, 9-5. IT/Ta

WINERIES OUTSIDE OF MAP AREA

THE FIRESTONE VINEYARD. 1 mi. N of jct. of U.S. 101 and Hwy. 154, 2 mi. E on Zaca Station Rd. (PO Box 244, Los Olivos 93441. Tel [805] 688-3940) Tours by appt.

KEY: GT (guided tour); IT (informal tour); Ta (tasting).

his property. Andrew York bought the winery in 1882 and passed it along to two more generations of Yorks.

It was here, incidentally, that Ignace Paderewski's Zinfandels were made into wine. (Paderewski loved the piano and the soil. But though he loved music first-hand, he preferred to keep farming at a respectable distance.)

In 1970 Max Goldman bought the handsome old brick winery and its vineyards with the notion of changing the specialty from Zinfandel to sparkling wine. The current owner has planted white grapes with that thought in mind.

Goldman, who has been a maker of sparkling wine in other parts of the country, put his first cuvee down for aging in the spring of 1975. The wine is scheduled to go to market in 1978.

While the new cuvees mature and remodeling of the cellar goes forward, visitors are invited to sample the still wines in a convivial tasting room that is naturally cool in summer and warmed by a gigantic fireplace in winter.

LODI

Dessert and table wines at the gateway to the Gold Country

When a wine industry official says "Lodi," he automatically takes in most of northern San Joaquin County, Sacramento and surroundings, and several bits and pieces of Sierra Nevada foothills. Using one town's name to cover all that territory is excusable shorthand. The 12 wineries right around the town of Lodi outnumber all others two to one. Several of them individually make more wine than all the distant relatives combined.

The town long was considered natural Sherry country, warm and dry through summer and well into fall. Until the early 1960s it produced far more dessert than table wine. Then, new grapes produced by the hybridizers at U.C. Davis helped reverse old habit, and Lodi started producing more table than dessert wine.

Sacramento, to the north, has a similar climate but a far less substantial involvement with grapes.

The Sierra foothills have another weather altogether. Late spring frosts are but one major aspect of a climate that makes grapes a dubious crop for investment. The gold miners of '49 were both thirsty and wealthy. Later generations have had to take a less optimistic, more businesslike view. Wine is a colorful but minor part of the Gold Country these days.

 LODI, TOWN AND COUNTRY

Lodi is a genuine Central Valley agricultural center. Most of its 29,000 population lives in tidily kept, tree-shaded residential districts around the main shopping area. Vineyards and other farmlands come right up to the edge. Grapes for table use, wine, and brandy constitute the major local crop.

Lodi nestles within the angle formed by the meeting of the Sacramento and San Joaquin rivers. Close to the rivers, conditions become too wet for grapes. East, the foothills impose their limits. The enforced compactness of Lodi may be its undoing if the town should ever grow to thrice its present population. Meantime, it works to the convenience of the visiting student of wine.

Even though the district is so compact that it can be driven edge to edge in 30 minutes, serious students will require two days to make a complete exploration.

The Wineries

For one reason or another, Lodi has been a focal point for wineries owned by cooperatives of grape growers. (Of its visitable wineries, two of the most visible belong to such organizations; another is owned by a conventional corporation; yet another is family owned.)

Whatever the pattern of ownership, the cellars form a fairly tight arc around the northeast quarter of Lodi town.

Barengo Cellars, known a bit less formally by local visitors as just Barengo's, looms up alongside Acampo Road in an expansive and rather pleasing brick building that formerly served as a grain barn.

In the year 1973 founder-proprietor Dino Barengo sold his winery, then immediately signed on for

WARMTH OF SPRING starts Lodi vines growing. By late summer, vines touch canes across the rows.

an extended term as winemaker to the new owners. They, in turn, have added substance to the premises without changing their character very much.

The original building houses a random assortment of upright redwood tanks, oak ovals, and small barrels strung out the length of an uncommonly long building. All the equipment has been gathered by Barengo.

The principal changes are two. First, the shed full of concrete fermenting tanks has given way to a battery of stainless steel fermentors. Second, the main cellar has been extended by a concrete block structure that houses the bottling line and cased wines waiting for shipment. (The cellar crew is particularly grateful for the new automatic bottling line, replacing one that could have served as the original inspiration for the Toonerville Trolley.)

Barengo's tasting room — brick walled, oak beamed, softly lighted — has two windows cut into its inside walls so visitors can keep an eye on the cooperage in the main aging cellar while exploring the wine list. The room evokes a fine bit of romance.

One of the winery specialties has been Ruby Cabernet, which Dino Barengo helped pioneer as a varietal wine. (It is an offspring of Cabernet Sauvignon and Carignane.)

The other specialties include these: a varietal dessert Sherry called Pedro Ximinez; a flavored after-dinner wine called Cremocha; and Dudenhofer May Wine, woodruff-flavored like the German model but distinct from it. More familiar varietal and generic table wines and appetizer and dessert types round out the list.

The name Barengo also is closely associated with wine vinegar, made in the traditional Orleans method in a separate building across the way from the winery. Veteran visitors will recall a low, boomerang-shaped building. Though it has been supplanted by a much larger concrete structure, the method remains as before. The hosts will explain making vinegar as patiently as they explain winemaking.

Coloma Cellars operates from an adobe-faced building on the State Highway 99 frontage road just north of Lodi.

Visitors to the small winery find a variety of table, dessert, and specialty wines available for tasting. There are no tours, either of the winery or of the adjacent building where grape concentrate is produced for home winemakers.

The label, incidentally, originated in a long-defunct cellar in the Gold Rush town of Coloma.

East-Side Winery, known by its label as Royal Host, has its tasting room inside a retired 50,000-gallon redwood wine tank.

The vessel, tailored to its new purpose with a man-sized door and interior varnishing, still gives a clear impression of how it feels to be inside a wine tank. It gives the optical illusion of being even bigger inside than outside.

The main winery buildings stretch southward from the roadside tasting room. As is often the case with cellars built in the 1930s, the architecture does not con-

BARENGO WINERY in Acampo welcomes company; its dark, cool tasting room offers many wines.

ONE-TIME WINE TANK now holds visiting tasters of East-Side Winery's long list of Royal Host wines.

form to romantic notions of a winery. Still, at East-Side the scenic deficiencies are only external. The interiors are full of handsome cooperage, all of it in admirably clean and orderly surroundings.

East-Side, as much as any winery in the district, reflects the increasing interest in making table wine. Members of the grower cooperative that owns it have responded strongly to the grape varieties developed at U.C. Davis; the Royal Host label appears on varietal bottlings of Emerald Riesling, Ruby Cabernet, and the rarer Gold. (Gold, a Muscat-derived grape, was originally intended to be eaten fresh, but it would not ship successfully. The wine resulting from it falls within the general classification of light, sweet Muscat.)

East-Side demonstrates equally well the lingering and probably unquenchable Lodi enthusiasm for making Sherry. In one building on the comprehensive tour is a large and informally organized Sherry solera.

After the tour, which is long, and the tasting, which can encompass a substantial list, visitors can retire to picnic tables just outside the tasting tank. On lawn, the tables are shaded by a mixture of tall trees. Family groups need give no advance notice, but larger groups are required to reserve in advance. The grounds will accommodate no more than 100.

Guild Wineries & Distilleries, largest producer of

wine among the state's cooperatives and one of the farthest flung associations of vineyardists, has its ancestral home and much of its presence in or near Lodi.

For visitors, the action is all at the central winery just off Victor Road (State 12) on the east side of town.

No wine is crushed on the premises. They are the aging and bottling facility. Like other firms engaged in trying to get great numbers of Americans to drink modestly priced wine as a daily dinner beverage, Guild finds itself required to have wines of many types. To meet this need, it must crush grapes of many varieties from sharply differing climate regions.

Two wineries in Lodi, two more near Fresno, and one at Delano do nothing but feed the bottling winery. In addition, Guild owns the Cresta Blanca winery at Ukiah (see page 26) and the Roma winery at Fresno (see page 101); the wines from both of these are brought to Lodi for bottling, too.

A modern, spacious, and cool tasting room called the Winemaster's House is out in front of the bottling cellars. Some who go to Guild limit their explorations to this oasis, especially when the summer sun heats Lodi into the 100° range or when winter rains pelt the countryside. However, the hosts willingly conduct tours in the worst of weathers as well as in the best.

Visible in the big cellars are concrete storage tanks of great capacity and steel tanks of still greater volume,

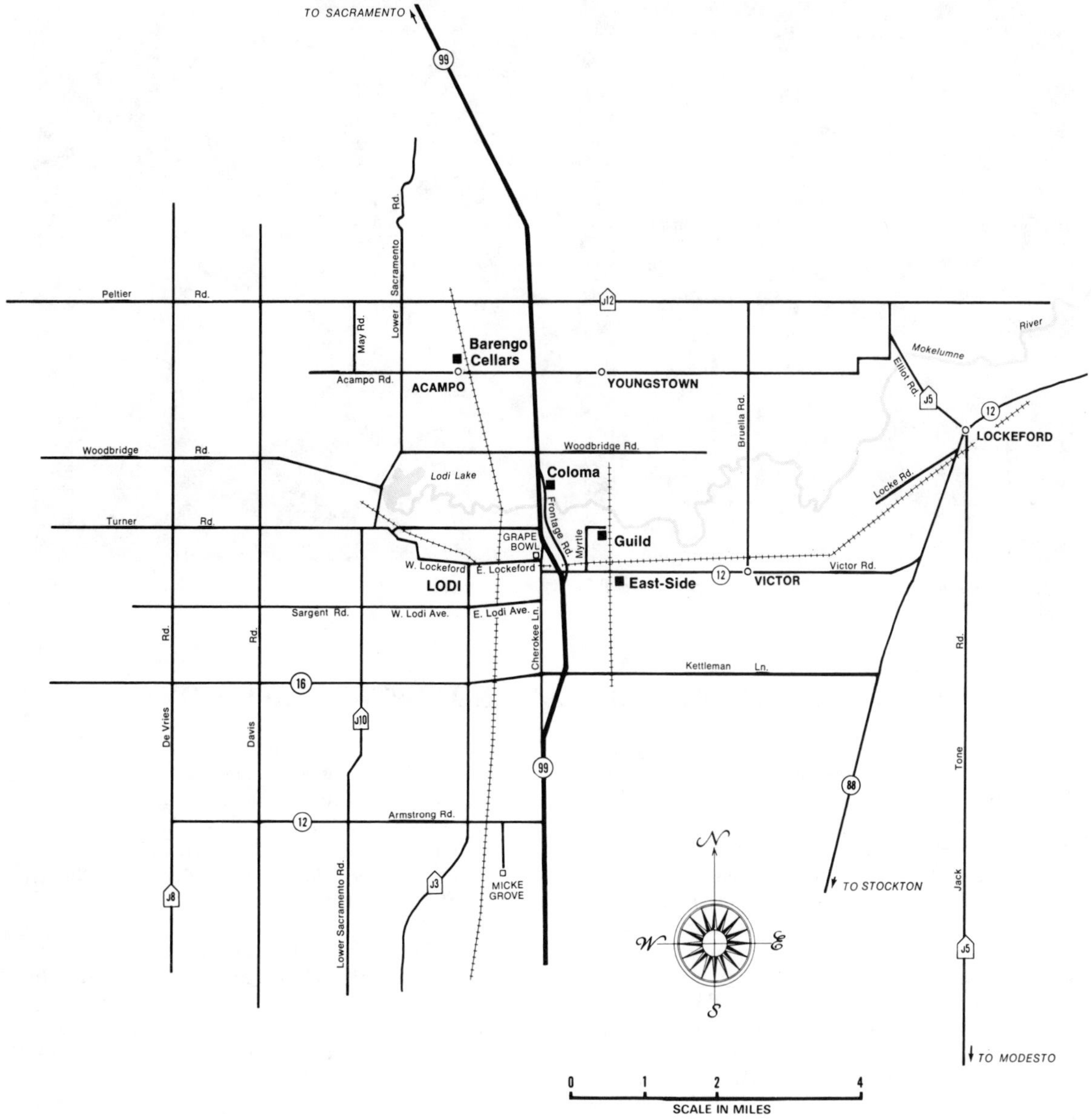

Map labels:
TO SACRAMENTO
99
Peltier Rd.
May Rd.
Lower Sacramento Rd.
Acampo Rd.
Barengo Cellars
ACAMPO
J12
YOUNGSTOWN
Mokelumne River
Elliot Rd.
J5
12
LOCKEFORD
Woodbridge Rd.
Woodbridge Rd.
Lodi Lake
Coloma
Bruella Rd.
Locke Rd.
Turner Rd.
Frontage Rd.
Myrtle
Guild
GRAPE BOWL
W. Lockeford E. Lockeford
12
Victor Rd.
LODI
East-Side
VICTOR
De Vries Rd.
Davis Rd.
Sargent Rd.
W. Lodi Ave.
E. Lodi Ave.
Cherokee Ln.
Kettleman Ln.
16
Tone Rd.
J10
99
88
12
Armstrong Rd.
Lower Sacramento Rd.
J3
MICKE GROVE
TO STOCKTON
Jack Rd.
J8
J5
TO MODESTO

N
W E
S

0 1 2 4
SCALE IN MILES

LODI

BARENGO VINEYARDS. From Hwy. 99, Acampo exit, W 1 mi. on Acampo Rd. (PO Box A, Acampo 95220. Tel [209] 369-2746) Daily, 9-5. GT/Ta

COLOMA CELLARS. N side of Lodi, cross Mokelumne River Bridge; on Frontage road, E side of S.R. 99. (PO Box 708, Lodi 95240. Tel [209] 368-7822) Daily, 9-5. Ta

EAST-SIDE (Royal Host). From S.R. 99 12-East exit, E 1 mi. (6100 E S.R. 12, Lodi 95240. Tel [209] 369-4768) Picnic. Daily, 9-5. GT/Ta

GUILD. From S.R. 99, Hwy. 12-East exit, E ¾ mi. to Myrtle Ave.; N ¼ mi. to winery drive. (PO Box 519, Lodi 95240. Tel [209] 368-5151) Picnic. Daily, 10-5. GT/Ta

KEY: GT (guided tour); IT (informal tour); Ta (tasting).

SOLERA'S oldest tier is refilled from next oldest. FLOR in a demonstrator cask.

SHERRY—DRY, MEDIUM, CREAM, AND FURTHER VARIATIONS

As a word, "Sherry" is not a great deal more precise than, say, "nuts." Both cover a vast ground (and they go well together).

The most noticeable difference from one Sherry to the next is in degree of sweetness. Some relatively dry ones are intended as appetizer drinks. Others, very sweet, come under the dessert category. In California the appetizer Sherries for the most part are labeled "dry" or "cocktail." The dessert types mostly go forth as "Cream Sherry."

Sherry begins being Sherry when the winemaker adds a bit of brandy to a newly fermented dry white wine. The purpose is to stabilize the wine so it will not turn to vinegar when it is exposed to oxidation, the next step. (Port differs. Its fermentation is stopped with brandy while a new red wine still has considerable sugar. The resulting wine is aged without being greatly oxidized.)

After this initial step, California winemakers produce their various Sherries in several ways, adding still more distinctions of flavor than sweetness.

Many "bake" it, though the word suggests more heat than they in fact apply. The usual limits are 120° to 140° for 45 to 120 days. Air space is left in the barrel or tank. Heat and air together produce the darkened color and characteristic flavor. Sweeter Sherries are made by blending an amount of Angelica or a similar wine after the base Sherry has been baked. The wine may or may not be aged further after baking.

The method, incidentally, originated in Madeira, Portugal, and is used to produce wines of that origin.

A variant method is long aging of partly filled barrels without the unusual warmth. In this instance oxygen and wood together form the flavor.

A radically different method involves cultivating a specific yeast as a film floating atop aging Sherry in a partially filled barrel or tank. The yeast, "flor," produces a distinctive flavor of its own. The yeast, oxidation, and the wood of the barrels all come together to form the characteristic flavors of this type of Sherry. In the case of flor Sherries, the initial addition of brandy is very slight and is augmented at the end of the aging period — which may be several years if the winemaker desires.

In California, several wineries use a variant method developed at the University of California. It is called "submerged yeast culture," an unromantic but accurate designation. Instead of a film of yeast being allowed to form and then work very slowly, a yeast is introduced into the wine and episodically agitated so it is present throughout the wine. The method, faster than film flor, produces a characteristic yeast flavor but without the wood flavor associated with film flors.

Whichever of these methods it uses, a winery may establish a "solera." Solera indicates only that a barrel is never emptied of all its wine. Rather, a certain fraction is removed for bottling, then a newer wine is added to the remaining part. In its most elaborate form, a solera may have several successive ranks, each filled from the next "youngest."

a complete Charmat Champagne cellar, a huge bottling room (that clanks and rattles at a furious enough pace to satisfy The Sorcerer's Apprentice), and, not least, the cased goods warehouse. There is an immense amount of wine at Guild, and the people there have worked out ingenious arrangements for dealing with it. For example, a sunken lane goes straight through the middle of the warehouse. It is just wide enough to accommodate flat-bed truck and trailer rigs and just deep enough for fork-lifts to drive right on and off the flatbeds to load them.

On an entirely separate plane, Guild maintains a dis-play vineyard adjacent to the Winemaster's House. In this vineyard the proprietors have planted three or four of each of the wine grape varieties recommended for California. Nowhere else can visitors see with so few steps how varied the vine is.

In the tasting room, Guild offers its full line of table, appetizer, dessert, and sparkling wines. Most are under the Winemaster's Guild label, but included prominently is the company's long-time trademark, the red and white checkered label of the Vino da Tavola wines. Guild also makes Famiglia Cribari.

Miscellaneous Wineries. In the course of poking around Lodi, one is bound to encounter other wineries. Most are marked by the tall towers that house their column stills (Lodi is a center for beverage brandy, as well as for the production of dessert wines).

One of the most striking wineries architecturally in the Lodi area is on Woodbridge Rd. at Bruella.

Once a bulk winery, Montcalm Vintners acquired it in the early 1970s and gave it an exterior facelift with a California mission theme. The family Filice owned it in 1975-76, but they, in turn, have now closed the winery doors.

The other Lodi wineries are purely in the bulk wine trade and not open to visit. They include Woodbridge Vineyard Association, Lodi Vintners, and Community Winery west of State 99, and Liberty Winery and Stock-ton Distillers' winery to the east. All are north of Lodi.

Other Than Wineries

The year-round attractions of the wineries are supple-mented by an annual festival with an uncommonly long name — the Lodi Grape Festival and National Wine Show. It takes place all over town on a weekend in mid-September, usually the one following Labor Day.

Most of the festivities are in the Grape Bowl, a fair-ground near State 99 northeast of Lodi. Wineries mount exhibits, and the local wine growers' association sponsors daily wine tasting in the midst of general farm displays and the most widely advertised feature of the festival, the grape mosaics.

The mosaics are what their name suggests — pictures or designs wrought by placing grapes one at a time on wire mesh. Sizes range up to panels 5 feet by 10. Club women spend hours plucking thousands of grapes and

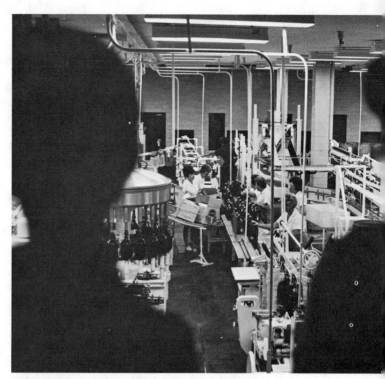

VISITORS to Guild Winery Central Cellar watch busy bottling line from raised walkway as tour finale.

FERTILE SOILS of Lodi district require several discings each season, one for each spring rain.

DUCKS IN THE DELTA FLYWAY cloud the wintry skies above Highways 4 and 12 for days during migration.

poking them into words and pictures that follow a pre-announced theme. (A typical motif is "Early California.") Grapes come in a wider range of colors than many people would suspect. The mosaics are as much a physiology lesson as they are an art study.

Elsewhere on the grounds concessionaires operate the usual quick food stands and carnival rides.

The main event is an hours-long parade with bands, floats, and drill teams. It assembles on the west side of town, winds through the business district, and finishes up 2 to 3 miles later under the summer sun at the Grape Bowl.

Everybody who is not in the parade watches it from a curbside vantage point and contributes to a formidable, postparade traffic tie-up. Agricultural communities lead more relaxed lives than manufacturing centers do, though, and all resolves itself in good-humored co-operation.

Several wineries hold open house during the festival just as they do all year. But they augment their staffs to run comprehensive tours for festival crowds that have numbered 50,000 to 60,000 in recent years.

Lodi also offers two recreational parks.

Lake Lodi Park, on Turner Road a mile west of State 99, rings the municipal lake, a diverted part of the Mokelumne River. Trees shade the shore and picnic tables. The park has rental boats and swimming beaches.

Micke Grove, south of town in a large stand of valley oaks, has a small zoo, gardens, and picnic sites. It is west of State 99 on Armstrong Road.

Plotting a Route

The town of Lodi straddles State 99, the quick route from almost any of the other San Joaquin Valley towns north or south.

For visitors coming from the San Francisco Bay region, the all-freeway route is Interstate Highway 580 through Livermore to Tracy, then north along the connector Interstate 205 to Interstate 5. To change from Interstate 5 to State 99 requires a brief descent onto some local road. Lathrop Road does the job as well as any. (It is about 4 miles north of the junction of Interstate 205 with Interstate 5.)

Another speedy route between the San Francisco Bay area — especially the northern half — and Lodi combines Interstate 80 as far east as Fairfield, then the two-lane State 12 from Fairfield to Lodi.

State 12 traverses a great deal of wine country. For the eastbound motorist, the road begins at Sebastopol, loops north through Santa Rosa and runs south in leisurely fashion through Sonoma town. From there it cuts east through the city of Napa and skims along the southern marches of Solano County until it joins Interstate 80 for a short run to Fairfield. From Fairfield it first passes through grassy hills, then along one slough and another in the Delta country until it straightens out and streaks for Lodi.

At one point the road offers an overview of the aircraft based at Travis Air Force Base. It also offers endless opportunities to study small boats while they pass the river bridge at Rio Vista.

A slower, somewhat more scenic variation of the Interstate 80-State 12 route between the Bay region and Lodi stays closer to the Sacramento River delta for a longer time. This route requires getting to the Contra Costa County town of Concord by whichever route is most efficient, then working east to Antioch on State Highway 4 and from there to Rio Vista along the levee road, State 160. At the Rio Vista Bridge, change to State 12 for the ride to Lodi.

Late fall or early winter, when great flights of ducks

HOW TO READ A CALIFORNIA WINE LABEL

Both California and federal laws control what a wine label must say.

Estate bottled. This once meant grapes from a single vineyard. Now it can cover the scattered holdings of large corporations.

1961. A vintage date can appear only if 95 percent or more of the grapes were harvested and crushed in the year stated. The margin allows for topping up casks of aging wines.

Napa Valley. Some statement of geographical origin is required. To be labeled "California," all of the wine must be from grapes grown in the state. More specific designations require 75 percent or more from the stated area.

Cabernet Sauvignon. Varietal labeling requires that 51 percent of the wine be from the grape named and that the wine get its predominant taste, aroma, and characteristics from that grape. Other labeling practices are generic (to describe a style of wine inspired by wine from a certain district, such as Burgundy or Sherry) and proprietary, a name coined by the vintner. See the chart on page 59 for a comprehensive list of California wines.

Produced and bottled by. This means the bottler made at least 75 percent of the wine by crushing, aging, and finishing.

Made and bottled by means the bottler was similarly responsible for 10 percent or more (in practice usually close to 50 percent). Terms like **Cellared and bottled by, Perfected and bottled by,** or **Prepared and bottled by** indicate only that the bottler performed some finishing procedures. Federal law requires as a minimum **Bottled by,** with the bottler's name and place of business.

Alcohol 12½ percent by volume. Table wines, 10 to 14 percent alcohol, may carry either a statement of alcohol content with a 1½ percent tolerance, or a statement such as "table wine" or "light wine." A statement of alcohol content is required on all dessert wines, with a tolerance range of 1 percent to the legal maximum of 21 percent.

---

darken the skies, has no peer as a season for driving between Antioch or Rio Vista and Lodi. Sometimes a tule fog comes in, rendering the day unsuitable for touring. But when the December or January weather is crisp and clear and the river runs full and the lines of trees have no leaf, few places in California tell a clearer story of the season. Even the farms in the bottom lands show no plants, only rich black soil, tilled and waiting for spring.

Spring can hardly be described as plain in these parts. The grasses wave long and green on every side. Cottonwoods and lesser trees brighten the riverbanks with fresh foliage. And local people turn out in numbers to fish for catfish in the sloughs, which are full to the brim — no more than a foot lower than the wheels of a car on the road — while farm crops on the dry side of the road wax healthy in ground a good 10 feet lower than the dike tops.

State 88 is one of the most scenic ways to get between State 49 in the Gold Country and State 99 down on the flat at Lodi. State 88 joins State 12 just west of the Camanche Reservoir, and the two proceed together through Lockeford into Lodi.

Going through Lodi to get to the Gold Country offers not only a scenic route but also a pleasant way to stop at one of the Lodi wineries for those who do not wish to make a specific visit for winery tours.

Within the neighborhood of Lodi, getting around requires little effort. West of State 99, Turner, Woodbridge, and Acampo roads serve well for east-west travel. The main north-south roads other than the freeway are De Vries and Lower Sacramento.

East of the highway, things spread out a bit more, but the same east-west roads (with the important addition of Victor Road) continue. The north-south roads are Kennefick and Bruella.

Within these grids the terrain is flat, given over mainly to vineyards but with occasional surprises, such as a line of olive or palm trees, an old dry river course with its bottom full of vineyard, or maybe a home garden.

A few vineyards are being trained up for trellising, a harbinger of mechanical harvesting; these are all young vines. A few are trellised in the ancient Italian style, almost like arbors, with trunks bare to head height. Still others — mostly very old Tokay vineyards — have six-foot-high vines, heavy and craggy and planted so close together that in winter, from even a slight distance, they appear to be a solid black mass.

GOLD RUSH began at Sutter's mill in Coloma.

AMADOR-EL DORADO

BOEGER WINERY. From Placerville E on Carson Rd. (1709 Carson Rd., Placerville 95667. Tel [916] 622-8094) Sa, Su, holidays, 10-5. Ta

D'AGOSTINI WINERY. From Plymouth, 8 mi. NE on Shenandoah Rd. (Rt. 2, Box 19, Plymouth 95669. Tel [209] 245-6612) Daily, 9-5. GT/Ta

GOLD HILL WINERY. Winery located on Cold Springs Rd., Coloma. Tasting room in Sierra Nevada House on W side S.R. 49, Coloma. (PO Box 267, Coloma 95613. Tel [916] 622-1712) Weekends only, 12-5. Ta

MONTEVINA. 3 mi. NE of Plymouth on Shenandoah School Rd. (Rt. 2, Box 30A, Plymouth 95669. Tel [209] 245-3412)

WINERIES OUTSIDE OF MAP AREA

COLUMBIA CELLARS (Tuolumne County). At S limit of Jamestown, W side of S.R. 108 & 49. (PO Box 629, Columbia 95310. Tel [209] 984-3727) Daily, 10-5. IT/Ta

KEY: GT (guided tour); IT (informal tour); Ta (tasting).

THE GOLD COUNTRY

One way and another, the miners of '49 courted wine. Some of the big winners in the gamble bought up vast amounts of it in their pay dirt celebrations in San Francisco or other parts. A good many who missed gold by direct digging went into business as wine merchants. A few went at it straightaway and planted vines on the spot.

The extent of 19th century vineyards in the Sierra is surprising. In 1880, for example, the Coloma Valley alone yielded half a million gallons of wine and brandy. But disease followed by disinterest wiped out nearly all of the pioneer vineyards before Prohibition.

With the wine boom of the late 1960s and early 1970s, vines began to creep back into the Sierra landscape in noticeable numbers.

One scientist at the University of California says that a Sierra foothill vineyardist, over the long haul, will harvest approximately 25 percent of what he might be entitled to expect in a normally favorable situation. Spring frosts and other vagaries of the weather will deprive him of the rest.

Short crops have not been enough to dissuade the hardy. Zinfandel in particular has become a favored vine in the region. Even though the roster of active local wineries has grown, some of the Zinfandel crop has been exported to the Napa and Santa Clara valleys to be made into wine there.

The Wineries

Five wineries presently are active in what must be called — for lack of a more precise term — the Gold Country. For the purpose, Gold Country includes Sierra foothills from Chico down to Sonora.

Widely separated, the wineries serve best as changes of pace rather than as prime touring goals.

The focal point, as much as there is one, lies in the rolling hills east of Plymouth town, in Placer County. A gentle swale there called the Shenandoah Valley has a considerable acreage of vineyards and a pair of relatively large wineries.

Boeger Winery, east of Placerville, revives a century-old winery property. Two stone structures survive from the 1870s when the winery and a distillery were established. No brandy is made these days, just table wine.

The winery is open weekends and tasting goes on inside the original stone winery building. Outside there is space to picnic.

ANTIQUE SHOPS are everywhere in the Gold Rush Country for nostalgic visitors to rummage through.

D'AGOSTINI WINERY is located in a long, narrow fold of the Sierra foothills called Shenandoah Valley.

Columbia Cellars opened in 1970 and moved to a new location in 1972. The current winery, a tiny one, is directly at the intersection of State 49 and State 108, handy to Columbia State Historical Park in the warm season or to Bear Valley and Dodge Ridge in winter.

Because it's a producing winery, it can offer informal tours of its working parts.

The tasting room is rustic by design.

D'Agostini Winery is the genuinely durable one in this lofty region. The first vines on the site east of Plymouth belonged to a Swiss named Adam Uhlinger, who planted them in 1856. For a good many years, Uhlinger made wine under his own label. The present owners, the D'Agostini family, bought vines and winery in 1911 and have been on the property ever since.

Uhlinger built for the long haul. He laid stone walls and strung heavy beams. The D'Agostinis have kept his handiwork intact, though the winery has prospered substantially and required a series of additions. They have also kept several of the oak casks that were coopered on the site by a neighbor of Uhlinger.

The buildings old and new are set at the foot of a gentle, vine-clad slope. Beyond the 125 acres of vineyard are hills wooded more thickly than is common in California wine districts.

Tours start with the fermentors and end with the tasting room. Burgundy and Zinfandel head the list of table wines.

Gold Hill Winery has a weekend tasting room adjacent to one of the restored old hotels of the Gold Rush Country, Sierra Nevada House.

The firm was founded in 1969 by John and Beverly Hempt, who planted vineyards of Chenin Blanc, Johannisberg Riesling, and Cabernet Sauvignon nearby. While these vines are growing up, the list of Gold Hill wines focuses on generics.

The winery proper is not open to visit.

Monteviña, the most sizable winery of recent vintage in the Gold Country, is managed by Cary and Vicki Gott for owner W. H. Field.

In essence, the up-to-date winery is an estatelike operation founded on the basic assumption that the Shenandoah Valley is a special region, particularly for the production of Zinfandel.

The 165-acre vineyard includes, first and foremost, Zinfandel. Other grapes planted for Monteviña varietal wines are Cabernet Sauvignon, Ruby Cabernet, Barbera, Sauvignon Blanc, and the rarely seen Italian grapes Primitivo and Nebbiolo.

At present only about a quarter of the total crop goes toward wine for the Monteviña label; other wineries buy the rest.

FRASINETTI cellar is an island of calm next to railroad tracks, at end of an industrial street.

Other Than Wineries

The Gold Rush Country, like much of the Wine Country, gains considerable appeal from having a romantic 19th century history. Yet the industry on which it was founded is now distantly past rather than flourishing and active. For a specific guide to the past and present of this golden countryside, see the *Sunset* book *Gold Rush Country*.

Plotting a Route

A plethora of state highways ascends from the San Joaquin Valley floor to intersect with State 49, the Gold Rush Country's north-south artery.

State 88, from Lodi-Lockeford to Jackson, ranks at the head of the list for scenic beauty with more than a few connoisseurs. It also has the advantage of arriving at the heart of an area tourable for souvenirs of the Gold Rush and for wineries.

There are other choices. U.S. Highway 50 from Sacramento is the fastest road of the lot, passing close to Coloma town. State 16 runs directly from Sacramento to Plymouth through agreeable countryside. State Highway 26 connects Stockton with San Andreas. State 4 runs between Stockton and Angels Camp. From the south, State 108 is a useful route from Modesto to Sonora.

Chico, lonely outpost of the vine, lies on State 99 a long way from all the rest of these places.

 ## SACRAMENTO

Sacramento is mainly the state capital, but it also has some enduring associations with the grape. Three wineries continue to function within or close by the city limits. One of the greatest ties, just a few minutes west on Interstate 80, is the Davis campus of the University of California. Davis is the home of the university's Department of Viticulture and Enology, one of the world's leading centers of research and training for grape growers and winemakers.

Wine touring in Sacramento, though, is not the day or weekend activity it can be elsewhere in the district. Here it's more of a respite from the road or an interval in some larger scheme.

The Wineries

Of the three wineries in or near Sacramento, only Brookside has a tour, and it is informal.

Brookside's Sacramento facility was founded as Mills Winery in 1910, had new owners in 1946, then became a part of the Southern California based Brookside Company in 1968.

A parchment document displayed in the tasting room attests to the winery's role in California history. The first railroad on the Pacific Coast was laid at the entrance to the winery property, and the Pony Express route used the adjoining property.

The winery is open daily for self-guided tours and tasting. A limited number of wines (mostly dessert) are still available by the barrel (an original distinction of Mills). All of the Brookside wines are available in fifths, half-gallons, and gallons.

Frasinetti and Sons dates back to 1897, a long career by local standards. Its founder, James Frasinetti, died at the age of 91 in 1965. His sons and grandsons continue the family tradition.

After the original building burned to the ground in 1924, it was replaced by a utilitarian collection of corrugated iron structures. During the early 1970s, the family added warm-hued stucco faces to the main cellar and the bottling building, made a handsome tasting room, and otherwise turned the property into a peaceable, even serene, island at the end of a busy industrial street running alongside the railroad right of way.

There is no tour, only tasting of a longish list of table and dessert wines. Two specialties are N B Tween (a dessert wine in between sweet and dry) and Cerasolo, a pale, soft red developed by the founder for those customers who found his regular reds too thick and dark.

Gibson Wine Company is a pioneer in the making and marketing of berry and fruit wines, but it also makes a range of table wines.

The winery was started in 1938 by Robert Gibson (who died in 1960) and continues under a cooperative ownership called Sanger Wine Association.

The great part of Gibson wine is shipped east in bulk to a bottling plant the company owns in Covington, Kentucky. But the proprietors do keep enough here to stock their tasting room.

The wines appear under three labels: Gibson's Old Fashioned for the fruit and berry wines, Gibson's Premium Select for the generic and varietal table wines, and Vinesse for the sparkling and dessert wines.

Vinesse also is the name of the tasting room, located several hundreds of yards south of the winery on the east side of State 99 at the Grantline Road exit.

The substantial winery is not open to tour.

Other Than Wineries

Though the Department of Viticulture and Enology at U.C. Davis is not open to the public, it deserves a bow from any appreciator of California wine who whistles past on Interstate 80 or cruises by on State 128 on the other side of the campus. The campus, 14 miles west of the capitol at Sacramento, is a pretty place to while away an hour or two in the midst of a great many trees and even more bicycles.

It would stretch matters to say that all of California technical progress in winemaking owes itself to the academicians at Davis, but the school had a lot to do with creating the spirit of enlightened inquiry that marks professional vintaging in the state. Its staff members are in demand among Australian, French, South African, and Yugoslav wine people, and others. They cooperate with their colleagues in other countries on technical counsel and guest instruction, and they serve as judges in international competitions.

The Davis faculty is also in demand at home, where it cooperates with the staffs at commercial firms on investigations of everything from disease-resistant rootstock to the abilities of different wines to age.

Some of the most visible results of the work at Davis are noted here and there throughout this book. But some of the most important results of the school's research will not be covered here because they have to do with

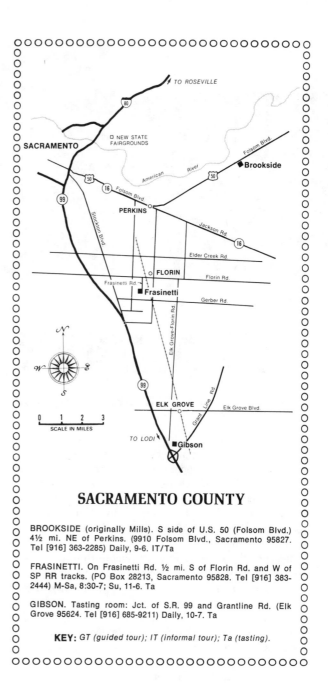

SACRAMENTO COUNTY

BROOKSIDE (originally Mills). S side of U.S. 50 (Folsom Blvd.) 4½ mi. NE of Perkins. (9910 Folsom Blvd., Sacramento 95827. Tel [916] 363-2285) Daily, 9-6. IT/Ta

FRASINETTI. On Frasinetti Rd. ½ mi. S of Florin Rd. and W of SP RR tracks. (PO Box 28213, Sacramento 95828. Tel [916] 383-2444) M-Sa, 8:30-7; Su, 11-6. Ta

GIBSON. Tasting room: Jct. of S.R. 99 and Grantline Rd. (Elk Grove 95624. Tel [916] 685-9211) Daily, 10-7. Ta

KEY: GT (guided tour); IT (informal tour); Ta (tasting).

such esoteric (but vital) matters as the roles of tannins in red wines or the tensile strengths of main stems in grape clusters.

Plotting a Route

Sacramento, being at the hub of Interstate 5, Interstate 80, and State 99, is not hard to find. Since the local wineries are fairly closely tied to the freeway system, getting to them is an easy task, as well.

The state capital is not vacation country, nor is it scenic vineyard country. There is little reason for wine buffs to explore local side roads.

SAN JOAQUIN

From Modesto to Bakersfield, America's largest vineyard district

No matter how it is approached, the San Joaquin Valley is vast. It's not wine country in a compact sense like the north coast counties, where a visitor can choose among half a dozen or a dozen wineries within a few miles. But in this far-flung agricultural empire, 35 wineries produce something like 65 to 70 percent of the state's annual volume of wine.

Because the valley towns are remote from the major coastal cities and because the valley has never become a vacation center in its own right, a good many of the wineries have not maintained visitor accommodations until recently. Now, increasingly heavy traffic on State Highway 99 and increasingly large local populations have persuaded more of the vintners to court visitors.

Except for people who have a head start because they live in the valley, the distances largely defeat one-day wine country tours. Some 200 miles of State 99 separate Modesto from Bakersfield; Modesto is 95 miles southeast of San Francisco; Bakersfield is 111 miles north of Los Angeles, and in all that space only 13 wine cellars had visitor facilities in the spring of 1975.

This doesn't mean there are no vinous charms for visitors from afar — only that these charms are more easily sought as interludes in longer journeys with more purposes than one.

MODESTO AND SURROUNDINGS

Modesto and the wine business didn't get together until the late 1930s. But the two have prospered together ever since. Modesto's population doubled in the 1950-1960 decade alone, bringing the count to 48,500. Though the production of wine has not increased quite that fast, it has progressed stoutly.

Nine wineries ring Modesto. Most of them — and all those that welcome visitors — are north, on one side or the other of the Stanislaus-San Joaquin county line. The nonvinous local attractions — mostly water-cooled parks — concentrate themselves in the foothills to the east, though the most accessible park is west of State 99.

The Wineries

It is no great distance from Lodi to Modesto, but in that few miles the pattern of winery ownership markedly changes. Lodi has a plethora of grower cooperatives and very few privately owned wineries. Modesto goes to the opposite extreme. In fact, there is not a co-op in the lot. But external appearances differ less.

Bella Napoli, Delicato Vineyards, and Pirrone Cellars are on or near the freeway. Cadlolo and Franzia are on State Highway 120 east of the freeway. (These two roads, connected by State Highway 108 for Escalon to Modesto, make a tidy winery-touring loop.)

Bella Napoli cannot encourage a tourist trade in the usual sense and has no tours and no tasting. The winery, at the rear of the family home, is in every respect a small, country enterprise.

For that reason Bella Napoli is evocative of an era that seems to be passing in the Central Valley faster than

RIVER BEND in the Kings River finds an echo in an immaculately tended vineyard north of Reedley.

in the coast counties. It is agreeable to stand in the court-yard, amid the whitewashed farm buildings, and nego-tiate a purchase when the dog quiets. The owners' family name is Hat — hardly as Neapolitan as they are.

Vines surround the place. Many are trellised. All are well tended. The far ends of the vine rows reach the foot of a tremendously long line of palm trees, a peculiarly Californian touch.

The label is Vine Flow, and all is table wine. The trade is mainly local, at the door.

Cadlolo Winery, in the town of Escalon, presents a fresh face to the world.

The main building of concrete and red brick looks almost new beneath its coat of pale cream paint. But it dates from 1913 when L. Sciaroni launched a winery on the site. Charles Cadlolo held the reins from 1937 to 1970. His sons, Raymond and Theodore, now own and operate the winery. The only signs that hint at the age of the winery are the old-style evaporative cooling tower on the roof and the mature tree that shades the front door.

Cadlolo's pride in the premises is evident in more than the fresh-painted appearance of the main building. The crusher, just alongside the winery, has a well-scrubbed air. The interior of the winery is equally tidy.

Tours, not quite formal, sometimes interrupted for a bit of work on the part of the guide, start at the crusher and go all the way through to the bottling department. Tasting is in a casual room just to one side of the main cellar, within sniffing range of the aromatic redwood

tanks of wine. Wines available include several generic table types and appetizer and dessert wines.

Delicato Vineyards occupies a very considerable plot of ground just alongside the southbound lanes of State 99 on a frontage road north of Manteca.

Signs give ample warning before the freeway exit onto what is very nearly a private lane. The winery has on each flank a residence of one or another branch of the owning family, the Indelicatos. (Given the family name, the proprietors must have taken great delight in naming the place Delicato. He who doubts the authenticity of the reverse twist has only to read the names on mailboxes on either side of the winery.)

Delicato has grown greatly during the past few sea-sons. A few years ago, an informal tour could cover all the ground within a small, iron-sheathed winery in a very few minutes. Now, formal tours launch out from a new-in-1975 textured block tasting room to take in impressive arrays of outdoor steel fermentors and storage tanks (al-most 6 million gallons worth), such esoteric contrivances as rotary vacuum filters, and the immaculately clean original cellar full of redwood tanks. The bottling line is the last stop.

The Delicato label covers a wide range of generic and varietal table wines, sparkling wines, and appetizer and dessert types.

Franzia Brothers is on State 120 east of Ripon. An attractively designed and furnished tasting room sits in the midst of a decorative block of vines next to the road.

CADLOLO OFFERS *wines by barrel or bottle from a well-maintained, sturdily built Escalon winery.*

HANDSOMELY HOUSED *tasting room at Franzia Brothers winery is restful stop on Yosemite Highway.*

The several large buildings of the winery proper stand farther back amid larger blocks of vines.

Giuseppe Franzia from Genoa established the family in the California wine business in 1906. The untimely intervention of Prohibition made it necessary that Giuseppe and five sons reestablish a Franzia winery in 1933. They did so with vigor. The winery was up to an annual production of 15 million gallons before the family sold the business in 1971. It now is owned by — of all people — the Coke folk.

Franzia wines include all of the familiar appetizer and dessert types, several sparkling wines, and a range of table wines. Most of the latter are generics. Some varietals were added to the list in 1974.

The company offers tours of its vast, mechanically efficient plant only by appointment. Appointments are generally limited to groups.

A tree-shaded picnic ground on lawns adjacent to the tasting room is open to casual drop-ins when it has not been reserved by groups.

Pirrone Wine Cellars, on the east side of State 99 just north of Salida's business district, is another of the small family enterprises (although it does not look especially small on the approach) that prospers among the industry giants.

Founder Frank Pirrone was an architect practicing in Garfield, New Jersey, when he bought some California vineyard acreage in 1923. Pirrone arranged to have an uncle manage the vineyard and sell its grapes to home winemakers until he finally managed to get west and build his own winery in 1936.

After his retirement two sons carried on for a time, selling wines in bulk. In 1964 Al Pirrone bought his

brother's share and began establishing his own label.

The main winery, built in 1946, is capable of handling a million gallons of wine annually. This is mainly dessert wine, and it goes in bulk to other wineries. Meantime, Pirrone buys selected lots of table wine for the tasting room from elsewhere in California.

The tasting room, entered through a 2,000-gallon upright tank set into the wall, has all Pirrone-label wines available for tasting, including the sparkling ones. The tasting takes place at a polished walnut bar mounted atop old barrel staves.

Informal tours of the winery allow the visitor to see the crusher, press, fermentors, and aging cellars at his own pace.

Miscellaneous Wineries. Aside from these wineries in which they are welcome, visitors to the Modesto area are likely to notice others.

By far the largest winery in Modesto, and perhaps in the world, is E. & J. Gallo. For the present at least it is not open to visit. Alas for that, because the Gallos have come from small and perfectly ordinary beginnings to a dazzlingly complex center for making wine under the most rational of conditions with the most efficient kinds of equipment. Nothing is left to wayward chance. The Gallos even have their own bottle manufactory on the premises, using glass made to their own patented formula.

Gallo made-on-the-spot bottles receive a complete range of generic table, sparkling, dessert, and flavored wines made from grapes grown the length and breadth of the state. The firm owns huge vineyard acreages in Modesto, Livingston, and in the Sierra foothills, buys more grapes on contract, and also buys the entire wine

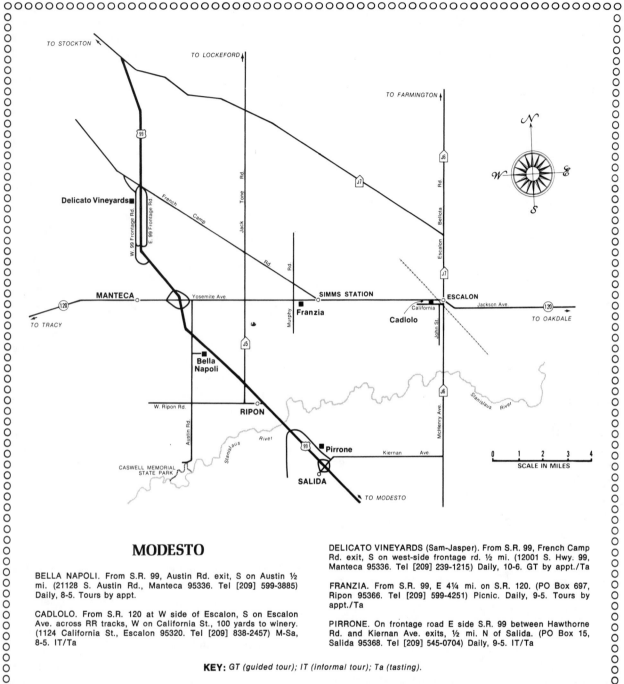

MODESTO

BELLA NAPOLI. From S.R. 99, Austin Rd. exit, S on Austin ½ mi. (21128 S. Austin Rd., Manteca 95336. Tel [209] 599-3885) Daily, 8-5. Tours by appt.

CADLOLO. From S.R. 120 at W side of Escalon, S on Escalon Ave. across RR tracks, W on California St., 100 yards to winery. (1124 California St., Escalon 95320. Tel [209] 838-2457) M-Sa, 8-5. IT/Ta

DELICATO VINEYARDS (Sam-Jasper). From S.R. 99, French Camp Rd. exit, S on west-side frontage rd. ½ mi. (12001 S. Hwy. 99, Manteca 95336. Tel [209] 239-1215) Daily, 10-6. GT by appt./Ta

FRANZIA. From S.R. 99, E 4¼ mi. on S.R. 120. (PO Box 697, Ripon 95366. Tel [209] 599-4251) Picnic. Daily, 9-5. Tours by appt./Ta

PIRRONE. On frontage road E side S.R. 99 between Hawthorne Rd. and Kiernan Ave. exits, ½ mi. N of Salida. (PO Box 15, Salida 95368. Tel [209] 545-0704) Daily, 9-5. IT/Ta

KEY: *GT (guided tour); IT (informal tour); Ta (tasting).*

production of grower cooperatives in the Central Valley, Sonoma, and Napa.

For the moment, it is possible only to drive past the headquarters in the southeast quarter of Modesto on Fairbanks Avenue.

In addition to the Modesto winery, the Gallos own two more at Livingston and Fresno.

United Vintners has a winery on State 120, about equidistant between Franzia to the west and the town of Escalon to the east. This, the original Petri winery, is not open to visit. (United Vintners welcomes tourists at its Asti winery in Sonoma County, see page 18, and at Inglenook in the Napa Valley, see page 36.)

Other Than Wineries

Modesto, unlikely as it may seem, is in the midst of a great deal of water. The Tuolomne and Stanislaus rivers join the San Joaquin just west of town. Folds in the hills just east harbor three major reservoirs.

Parks in and around Modesto are designed to beat the summer heat, which almost daily tops 90° from mid-June into early October. Residents make the point that low humidity renders it a bearable kind of heat, but the parks are still in the shade and along the water.

West of Salida, Caswell State Park extends 4 shaded miles along the Stanislaus River. The river, shallow here, has a number of swimming holes. Picnic sites under spreading oaks are 10 to 15 degrees cooler than nearby farm fields. Head west from State 99 on Austin Road. The exit is 2 miles south of Manteca. The park, 5 miles west of the highway, is the only one close to wineries.

Each of the major towns in the district also has a municipal park for quick picnics.

Plotting a Route

All of the wineries open to visit in the Modesto area are located on State 99 or State 120, two roads that form an awkward, toppling "T."

On the San Joaquin Valley floor, these and all other roads are flat, with few or no curves.

The visual interests are subtleties on a vast canvas. A shift from row crop to orchard is gross change, especially when February and March light the orchards with blossom. Random occurrences of single oaks or small clusters in the fields produce eerie perspectives on a misty day. There is a prodigious number of unpainted, decaying small barns to consider in this era of large-scale agriculture. Residential architecture ranges from a rare brick colonial to a profusion of board-and-batten cottages.

For visitors coming into the valley from the sea side of the Coast Ranges, the efficient route is to follow Interstate 580 from the San Francisco Bay area to Tracy, then State 120 from Tracy to Manteca.

For those coming from south of San Francisco, State 132 connects Interstate 5 with State 99 at Modesto. State 132 is wide and quick.

 FRESNO

The highest point in Fresno is the 20th floor of its Rodeway Inn. Look out from that floor on a typical heat-hazy day in summer, and no hill of stature will appear in view. Fresno is flat.

Yet it manages to have charms. The main street of Fresno's original business district, fading a few years ago, has been turned into a spacious shopping mall with fountains, many trees (and shaded sitting places), and 20 specially commissioned sculptures. Nearby, a new convention center of unusual architecture is the stage for attractions both home-grown and imported.

To the north of the original city center, West Shaw Avenue has become a long, often architecturally distinc-

tive sequence of shopping centers and office buildings.

The central city may have begun to acquire a certain urbanity in this era of large-scale and mechanized farming (everybody in the Central Valley calls it "agribusiness" these days), but Fresno is, nonetheless, a farm center. The talk in the coffee shops has to do with one crop or another.

Among those crops, grapes figure most prominently. Fresno and neighboring counties north and south produce enough raisins for the Western Hemisphere and enough table grapes for much of the United States. In recent years the district's share of wine production has slipped below its old level of 50 percent of all California wine, but only because other districts have added vineyards more rapidly than has Fresno.

Traditionally the production has leaned toward Sherries, Ports, Muscats, and other sweet dessert wines. The long, sunny summers favor sugar-laden grapes with their ancestral roots in Portuguese or Spanish soils. Here, as in Lodi and Modesto, specially developed warm-climate grapes for table wines are replacing other varieties or supplementing them.

Reading the founding dates of wineries, an innocent man might assume that winemaking did not get going in Fresno until 1936 or so, as in the case of Modesto. Blame Prohibition for creating yet another false impression. A man named Lee Eisen planted the first vineyard in the district in 1873. (Three rail-sitters of the day volunteered to eat the entire crop, which they might have done the first year but never thereafter.) Grapes have flourished in Fresno from Eisen's time on, and a good many have gone into wine since 1876.

The Wineries

The Fresno district covers an awesome number of square miles from Madera on the northwest to Cutler on the southeast. Within that vast expanse, fewer than a dozen wineries welcome visitors. But sparse as the numbers might be, the wineries are of such diverse character as to make a complete sampler of everything from giant to miniature, from generalist to specialist, from ultramodern to entirely traditional.

California Growers dates from 1936, one of many grower cooperatives in the San Joaquin Valley with its birthdate in the immediate post-Prohibition era.

Growers was then and is now a kind of distant outpost of big valley wine, nestled against the east hills at the town of Cutler, about 25 miles due east of Kingsburg.

The co-op is producing and bottling wines under its own "Growers" and the affiliated "Setrakian" labels. Growers covers a full range of table and dessert wines. Setrakian labels go on a longish list of varietals, including Chenin Blanc, Semillon, Barbera, Ruby Cabernet, and Zinfandel.

For the time, the winery has neither tours nor tasting, only retail sales.

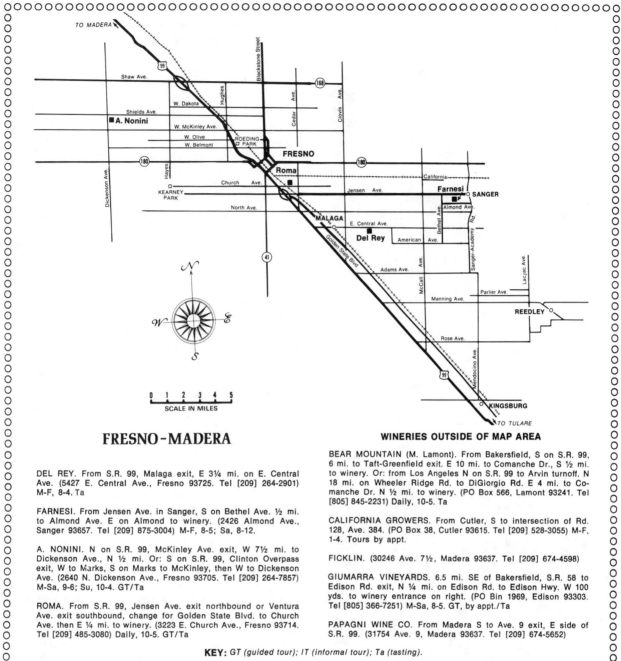

FRESNO-MADERA

DEL REY. From S.R. 99, Malaga exit, E 3¼ mi. on E. Central Ave. (5427 E. Central Ave., Fresno 93725. Tel [209] 264-2901) M-F, 8-4. Ta

FARNESI. From Jensen Ave. in Sanger, S on Bethel Ave. ½ mi. to Almond Ave. E on Almond to winery. (2426 Almond Ave., Sanger 93657. Tel [209] 875-3004) M-F, 8-5; Sa, 8-12.

A. NONINI. N on S.R. 99, McKinley Ave. exit, W 7½ mi. to Dickenson Ave., N ½ mi. Or: S on S.R. 99, Clinton Overpass exit, W to Marks, S on Marks to McKinley, then W to Dickenson Ave. (2640 N. Dickenson Ave., Fresno 93705. Tel [209] 264-7857) M-Sa, 9-6; Su, 10-4. GT/Ta

ROMA. From S.R. 99, Jensen Ave. exit northbound or Ventura Ave. exit southbound, change for Golden State Blvd. to Church Ave. then E ¼ mi. to winery. (3223 E. Church Ave., Fresno 93714. Tel [209] 485-3080) Daily, 10-5. GT/Ta

WINERIES OUTSIDE OF MAP AREA

BEAR MOUNTAIN (M. Lamont). From Bakersfield, S on S.R. 99, 6 mi. to Taft-Greenfield exit. E 10 mi. to Comanche Dr., S ½ mi. to winery. Or: from Los Angeles N on S.R. 99 to Arvin turnoff. N 18 mi. on Wheeler Ridge Rd. to DiGiorgio Rd. E 4 mi. to Comanche Dr. N ½ mi. to winery. (PO Box 566, Lamont 93241. Tel [805] 845-2231) Daily, 10-5. Ta

CALIFORNIA GROWERS. From Cutler, S to intersection of Rd. 128, Ave. 384. (PO Box 38, Cutler 93615. Tel [209] 528-3055) M-F, 1-4. Tours by appt.

FICKLIN. (30246 Ave. 7½, Madera 93637. Tel [209] 674-4598)

GIUMARRA VINEYARDS. 6.5 mi. SE of Bakersfield, S.R. 58 to Edison Rd. exit, N ¼ mi. on Edison Rd. to Edison Hwy. W 100 yds. to winery entrance on right. (PO Bin 1969, Edison 93303. Tel [805] 366-7251) M-Sa, 8-5. GT, by appt./Ta

PAPAGNI WINE CO. From Madera S to Ave. 9 exit, E side of S.R. 99. (31754 Ave. 9, Madera 93637. Tel [209] 674-5652)

KEY: GT (guided tour); IT (informal tour); Ta (tasting).

Del Rey Cooperative Winery Association, as its name makes clear, is another grower co-op, founded in 1945. Through the 1950s the Del Rey growers marketed all their wines in bulk to neighboring wineries. In recent years they have moved to establish their own brand (Rancho Del Rey). It includes both table and dessert wines (Burgundy, Sauterne, Rosé, Muscat, Port, Sherry).

With the establishment of its own brand, Del Rey opened its first tasting room in 1974. The room is a one-time Pullman car, parked in front of the buildings that house the winery and repainted to read Rancho Del Rey.

There are no tours of this winery, designed as it is to be functional rather than fancy.

Farnesi Winery in Sanger is a small family enterprise founded in 1935 by a transplanted Tuscan named Corado Farnesi and carried on since 1951 by his nephew Danny Farnesi. The younger Farnesi, having had the benefits of practical instruction from his uncle and academic work at Fresno State College, runs the winery alone in all seasons except for the vintage one. Then the whole family joins in to make two red table wine types and one white.

ONE-TIME LUXURY railroad car has found a second career as the tasting room at Del Rey winery.

The winery, in a wooden barn across the street from a row of tidy residences, requires no tour. The proprietor will talk shop over a cordial glass.

Ficklin Vineyards, out of Madera, is one of the smallest wineries in the Central Valley, and certainly the most single-minded.

The specialty is a Tinta Port entirely from four selected Portuguese grape varieties. Not only the specialty, it is nearly the sum of winery production. The owners started making Emerald Riesling and Ruby Cabernet table wines for their own amusement a few years ago and have come to market a very few bottles of each, but this remains a casual part of the enterprise.

The Ficklin family enterprise dates back to 1911, when Walter Ficklin arrived in the Fresno area and immediately launched into grape cultivation and other fruit growing. Wine entered the picture in the early '40s when scientists at the University of California at Davis encouraged growers to plant several Portuguese grape varieties that had shown promise in tests.

David Ficklin, after studying at Davis, began as the winemaker and continues in that role. He also manages the winery. Walter Ficklin, Jr. is the vineyardist.

The winery was founded in 1946, and in 1948 the first wine was made from Tinta cao, Tinta Madeira, Alvarelhao, and Touriga grapes.

The main cellar, small and low in a flat sea of vineyards west of State 99, has walls of adobe brick fashioned by the family on the site. It is, on its own, a tribute to the traditional bent of the Ficklins. Still, they are only bent toward tradition, not bound by it. They have, for example, abandoned their original concrete fermentors in favor of more practical steel tanks. And they have abandoned binning their bottled wines in favor of storing them in their case boxes so the wines do not have to be handled so often.

Against those changes, the Ficklins age their wines in traditional small oak cooperage as they have done since their first vintage.

The Ficklins sell their Emerald Riesling and Ruby Cabernet, along with the Tinta Port, in the retail room. Happen along when the time is right, and one of the special bottlings of vintage Port may be on hand. From 1948 through 1957, the Ficklins selected casks from 4 years for vintage dating. Since then, they reluctantly have passed up two or three superior vintages for lack of enough wine to reserve, but the hope remains to resume with vintages.

Because the winery is a tiny family affair, the proprietors request appointments before visits. They will explain how to find the well-hidden premises when you set the time for a visit.

A. Nonini Winery, on the west edge of Fresno, was founded in 1936 by A. (equally appropriate for Antonio and Angiolina) Nonini and has since passed to the hands of three sons, Geno, Gildo, and Reno. The third generation is now entering the family winemaking arena.

TINY FICKLIN cellar nestles into a grove of trees amid vine rows south and west of Madera town.

Since the Noninis own all their own grapes, they lay claim to having the only estate-bottled wines in Fresno County. The production is limited to table wines.

The tour of the premises takes in every step from vineyard to bottling, ending up in a fittingly informal tasting room. Along with Bella Napoli, Cadlolo and Farnesi, this is one of the last four survivors of the once-abundant family wineries of the San Joaquin. The number of these places has perhaps diminished with time, but the flavor of this one has not. It is the pure article.

Angelo Papagni vineyards and winery, tucked into one corner of a freeway cloverleaf just south of Madera, is, in 1975-76, still refining its basic construction.

Full-fledged tour and tasting facilities are in the future. Meanwhile, the impressively modern winery is open to visit by appointment. At those times when wines are being tasted in the labs, visitors may be invited to join in.

A tour takes in a crushing facility that rivals the nearby cloverleaf for size and design, as well as steel and wood aging cellars. The wines include Barbera, Alicante Bouschet, a rare red Grenache, and Muscats.

Roma Winery, since its 1970 acquisition by Guild Wineries & Distilleries, has blossomed into an eminently visitable property.

Beginning at the beginning, the proprietors took a huge, brick-walled aging cellar, removed the tanks from it, and turned it into the visitors' reception and tasting room. Fanciful flags and pennants hang from the lofty ceiling and tall walls. Soft couches crop up at several points, and a spacious tasting bar runs along all of one wall and most of another.

Guides launch out on hourly tours from this point. The way stops include Roma's huge crushers, an aging cellar full of big redwood tanks, another cellar with 120-odd oak oval casks ranging up to the improbable size of 6,500 gallons, and — unique in all California — a close-up look at the column stills in the brandy cellars.

The walk is a long one, out of the tasting room onto B Street, along it as far as Fourth, then back. (When John Cella was developing Roma in the post-Prohibition era, he meant to have a giant of a winery. The fact that the place is laid out on a grid of streets suggests that he achieved his goal. Roma is not gigantic these days, but it is big, and sprawls more than many newer places.)

Miscellaneous Wineries. Another nine wineries operate in the general area. They are these: California Products, Sierra, Vie-Del, and Viking in Fresno; Lucerne in Hanford; Mission Bell (United Vintners) in Madera; Cella (United Vintners) and Mt. Tivy (The Christian Brothers) in Reedley; and Selma in Rio Vista. None has visitor accommodations of any sort; they do not even sell wines at retail.

Other Than Wineries

Fresno has two excellent parks and a mysterious underground grotto as alternate diversions to winery tours.

INSIDE MAIN CELLAR, Roma tasting room is a veritable carnival of colorful appointments.

LONG, TALL façade of main Roma cellar only hints at the overall size of this sprawling winery.

Roeding Park, 157 acres tucked between the freeway and State 99-Business and between Olive and Belmont Avenues, is a tree-shaded, quiet respite from the valley sun. There are several areas for children, including a storyland, a zoo, and an amusement arcade. You'll discover rental boats for paddling about a sizable pond, and spacious picnic areas beneath tall rows of eucalyptus.

Kearney Park is 7 miles west of Fresno on Kearney Boulevard. It is a huge, county-operated picnic park on the grounds of the old M. Theo Kearney estate. Several large areas are set aside for group reservations. Interspersed between these are a great many small areas for first-come family use.

The mysterious underground grotto of Baldasare Forestiere is north of Fresno, two blocks west of State 99 on Shaw Avenue. Forestiere was a Sicilian possessing Herculean powers with a pick and shovel. After digging for 38 years, he ended up with a maze of tunnels that runs beneath 7 acres of surface ground. The deepest rooms are 25 feet below ground and 20 degrees cooler than summery afternoons up top.

Plotting a Route

For people already in the San Joaquin Valley, State 99 is the obvious means of approaching Fresno-area wineries from either north or south. Anyone starting from the San Francisco Bay area can get across the coast ranges most efficiently on Interstate 580, though State 152, the Pacheco Pass Highway, is more scenic and only slightly slower.

In addition to being the basic approach route, State 99 is also a useful thread in getting from one winery to another since it makes a long, diagonal slice through the region that somewhat parallels the sequence of cellars.

Generally speaking, none of the roads leading you to a chosen winery door provides stunning scenery. The possible exceptions would be those roads in the Reedley-Sanger district that get close to the course of the Kings River. These lead you past changing terrain and brightened colors.

 BAKERSFIELD

Kern County has long been a raisin and table grape-growing district. After 1969 it began to be a very considerable wine grape-growing region, as well.

The impetus came from the general wine boom of the era. The potential came from hot climate grapes developed at the University of California at Davis, from new training methods for old varieties, and from the availability of irrigation water.

Only two wineries open their doors to visitors in the usual sense of the word. Both are east of town.

Bear Mountain was the earliest winery to make special use of the new wine grape plantings in Kern County, primarily under its M. LaMont label.

The list of varietal table wines is a roll call of the grape varieties known to be suited to the warm valley climate: Chenin Blanc, Emerald Riesling, French Colombard, and Semillon among whites; Grenache for rosé,

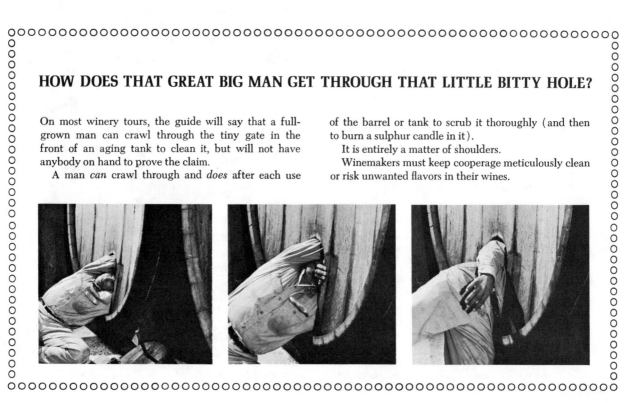

HOW DOES THAT GREAT BIG MAN GET THROUGH THAT LITTLE BITTY HOLE?

On most winery tours, the guide will say that a full-grown man can crawl through the tiny gate in the front of an aging tank to clean it, but will not have anybody on hand to prove the claim.

A man *can* crawl through and *does* after each use of the barrel or tank to scrub it thoroughly (and then to burn a sulphur candle in it).

It is entirely a matter of shoulders.

Winemakers must keep cooperage meticulously clean or risk unwanted flavors in their wines.

CONICAL PEAK *called Bear Mountain looms up behind the sprawling winery named after it.*

and Barbera, Ruby Cabernet, and Zinfandel for reds.

The company had been around for some years as a cooperative dealing in bulk wine when its members decided to begin bottling the best of their annual production as M. LaMont. The new label first appeared in 1972; the winery opened its doors to public visit soon after. (The winery is a namesake of Bear Mountain, the symmetrical peak that looms above and beyond the buildings. M. LaMont is a name borrowed from the nearest town up the road.)

For a time the company conducted tours of its rambling collection of outdoor steel tanks and cellar buildings. Since the walks were too long in summer heat or winter chill, though, the proprietors developed a film of the annual cycle of winemaking. They now show how all is done to visitors who remain comfortably seated in the spacious tasting room. There is ample opportunity to sense the scope of a large winery during the drive up its private lane to the tasting room.

This, incidentally, is the only tasting room in the state with an airstrip right next to the front door. Because the strip is private, fly-in visitors must write ahead to the Public Relations Director for a "hold harmless" form.

Giumarra Vineyards, a family firm, began producing varietal table wines under the family name in 1974 after a long career in the bulk trade. Like Bear Mountain, the winery added visitor facilities to signal the event.

The Giumarra winery occupies the farthest end of a sizable complex of buildings near Edison. Other structures house table grape packing operations and other facets of a multifarious farming business. It takes several minutes to drive from the entrance down to the sculptured concrete building that houses visitor facilities.

The tasting room, on the second floor of an ultra-modern bottling hall, allows visitors to watch work in progress while they sample Chenin Blanc, Emerald Riesling, Barbera, Ruby Cabernet, and Petite Sirah (among the table wines) and several Sherry and Port types, as well.

Guides give a short walking tour of the crushing area and aging cellars when time allows.

Miscellaneous Wineries. Bakersfield and nearby towns have several other wineries but none open to tour in the general sense. A. Perelli-Minetti & Sons at Delano has as labels Ambassador and Eleven Cellars but does not maintain even a retail shop at the large, family-owned winery. California Mission Wines at MacFarland and Delano Growers Cooperative at Delano sell all of their wines in bulk.

Relentless students of California winemaking may, with effort, be able to arrange for special tours at one or two of these wineries. The most efficient way is through the Delano Chamber of Commerce, attached to the Kern County Board of Trade in Bakersfield.

LOS ANGELES

Who'd suspect 12,000 acres of vines exist an hour from downtown?

Time and the restless tide of population in Southern California have caused a whole series of great shifts in the vineyards of this oldest of California's winegrowing regions.

Jean Louis Vignes planted the first commercial vineyard in what is now downtown Los Angeles as early as 1831.

At present the greatest concentration of vines is in the area east of Los Angeles, between the towns of Ontario and Fontana. But as population pressures grow more severe with each passing year, vineyards continue to suffer a space squeeze.

In searching for new land to plant, several vineyardists have turned south to Rancho California in Riverside County, where they have found much cooler growing conditions than those in Cucamonga.

In spite of the shifting focus in the vineyards, most of the touring activity south of the Tehachapis concentrates itself in Cucamonga, where the local wineries are among the busiest in the state in welcoming visitors.

 EAST OF LOS ANGELES

A wide, relatively unpopulated strip runs north and south between Ontario and Fontana. Within it lies nearly all of the present-day Cucamonga wine district.

Cucamonga hardly exists as a specific place. It is an intersection of Archibald Avenue and Foothill Boulevard—or a post office. The more general description of the area these days would be Pomona Valley. But wine goes back to the 1830s in Cucamonga, and that will be the name of the wine district for as long as it endures.

Whatever it's called, this is a curious countryside. The San Gabriel Mountains rise sharply, in effect forming a wall on the north side of the valley. At the foot of the mountains, a gently sloping and remarkably even alluvial fan runs better than a mile before it flattens and becomes the true valley floor. Farther south a less imposing range of hills called the Jurupas marks a tentative limit. If you fly into Ontario airport when the winds are westerly, the final approach pattern crosses over block after block of vines. Back on the ground, though, when you drive through the countryside, it turns out that a great many of the vineyards have for-sale signs on the corners and have not recently been harvested.

Industry and population press in together from east and west. A few years ago San Bernardino County had 23,000 acres in bearing vines. By 1972 the figure had dwindled to 12,000 acres. The buyers of many of those acres have left the vines to die as they await a day of better prices.

Still, 12,000 is a great acreage, and the history of the vine is long and strong in this district. It has been a habit in Cucamonga to play the part of the traditional country winery and to sell at the cellar door. Even the larger cellars in the district have sold much, if not all, of their wine this way. This trend only increases. The major companies have gone out and built more cellars as a means of having more doors in favorable locations. It is but one more economic advantage for them in a time of ever-rising costs.

TOWERING EUCALYPTS, *squat vines march together frequently in the flat reaches of Cucamonga.*

The Wineries

For the moment there is a diversity of choice in wineries to visit in that north-south axis between Ontario and Fontana. Two good-size firms offer extensive tours. So do a couple of smaller ones. Several of the wineries also have tasting rooms scattered throughout the area.

Brookside Vineyard Company says it is in Guasti. In fact, it nearly *is* Guasti.

The winery buildings are numerous and spread out over an uncommonly large plot of ground. The freeway called Interstate Highway 10 sets limits to the north, Turner Road to the east, A Street to the south, and Archibald Avenue to the west.

The vineyard stretches west. Across A Street is the main runway of Ontario's airport. To the east the parish church, somber, Italian, handsome, looks across from its lonely vantage point on the other side of Turner Road.

Within this ample area, visitors can spend a good deal of time getting to all the potential stops. The beginning is the southwest corner of Brookside, near the intersection of A and Archibald, where tours depart from the stone-walled tasting room and retail store building. Weekdays, signs do the guiding. Weekends, a host (or hostess) leads the way.

The main winery is a startling structure. The end walls — with their looping curves — suggest Mediterranean inspiration. Built of a dark gray river rock that must have been abundant here once, the walls measure better than 3 feet thick. The overall dimension of the building is 100 by 600 feet. Inside, an underground aging cellar is of proportionate size.

The family maintains a grassy, tree-shaded patch just across a parking lot from the tasting room. It has picnic tables to accommodate 30 persons on a first-come basis and is spacious enough for at least that many again to spread cloths on the ground.

During the second weekend in October, Brookside sponsors a local harvest festival. The main event is a blessing of the crop, which follows a High Mass at the parish church. The church, San Secundo d'Asti, is named as a tribute to Secundo Guasti, whose initiative led to its founding. After the blessing of the grapes, picnicking and folk dancing begin at the winery grounds.

Although Brookside traces its own history back to 1832, its owners did not set the architectural style at Guasti. It stems from Secundo Guasti, who originally built a winery called Italian Vineyard Company on this site at the turn of the century. Brookside first moved to Guasti in 1916 and resumed operation in 1952 after a lapse of several years.

The earlier history of the Brookside enterprise is pretty much a family affair. A French emigrant named Théophile Vaché planted vines in the Monterey region in 1832. His heirs moved to Redlands in the 1880s and employed another expatriate Frenchman, Marius Biane, who, as things often go in California's French-owned wineries, married the boss's daughter. Descendants of that marriage, the third generation of Bianes, now carry on the family history at the enterprise in Guasti.

Once the sole owners, the Bianes sold the winery to

BEFORE BOTTLING, wines rest in small barrels at Brookside's winery. The cellar is underground.

CUCAMONGA WINES slumber in 11,000-gallon redwood upright tanks in an archetypal cellar scene.

Beatrice Foods, Inc., and now serve as managers.

The current story is one of expansion. In 1968 Brookside acquired the old Mills Winery, which had developed a chain of tasting rooms in Northern California. Since then, the firm has gone on to open still more tasting rooms in California and in other states. The total has long since passed 30.

Wines on hand in the tasting and retail rooms are labeled Brookside, Assumption Abbey, and Vaché. The middle label resulted from the Bianes' agreement to produce sacramental wines to meet needs of the Benedictine order of monks.

Under one or more of those labels, Brookside offers a wide range of table, appetizer, dessert, and sparkling wines. The table wines include such oddly named entries as Dido Noir and Saint Emilion, along with many more familiar appellations.

Current Assumption Abbey wines emphasize varietals from the Biane Vineyards on Rancho California, near the town of Temecula. The Bianes were among the first growers in that region.

Callaway Vineyards and Winery marks a new turn in winemaking south of the Tehachapi Mountains — a pioneering shift toward a small, estatelike winery producing only varietal table wines.

Occupying a series of rolling knolls in Rancho California, the winery and vineyards are the property of retired business executive Ely Callaway. The winery was founded in 1973 amid vines planted in 1969.

Astute students of winemaking equipment will find surprises in and alongside the metal-walled building. Notice, for example, a continuous press and a centrifuge. Both pieces of equipment usually are found in cellars much larger than this one. Otherwise, the stainless steel fermentors and small oak cooperage are of much the same type as those found in similar-size wineries in Napa or other northerly counties.

Callaway wines include Johannisberg Riesling, Sauvignon Blanc, Chenin Blanc, Cabernet Sauvignon, Petite Sirah, and Zinfandel.

Because the winery is a tiny one, visitors are encouraged to come in groups and must come with appointments. Tastings are arranged as part of group tours.

Louis Cherpin Winery is housed in a main building that has undergone intermittent expansions ever since its foundation stone went down in 1934. The successive enlargements are marked by changes from brick to red block to concrete block.

Large vines are trained up each section. Inside, most of the cooperage is upright redwood. In early 1968, when the Adelanto Winery closed its doors forever, the Cherpin brothers bought several oak ovals that had been coopered in Germany on special order for the former owners. These now line one wall of the winery alongside the bottling equipment.

The winery, flanked by several frame outbuildings and equipped with an honor guard of various dogs (all friendly), is at the end of a short dirt drive off Valley

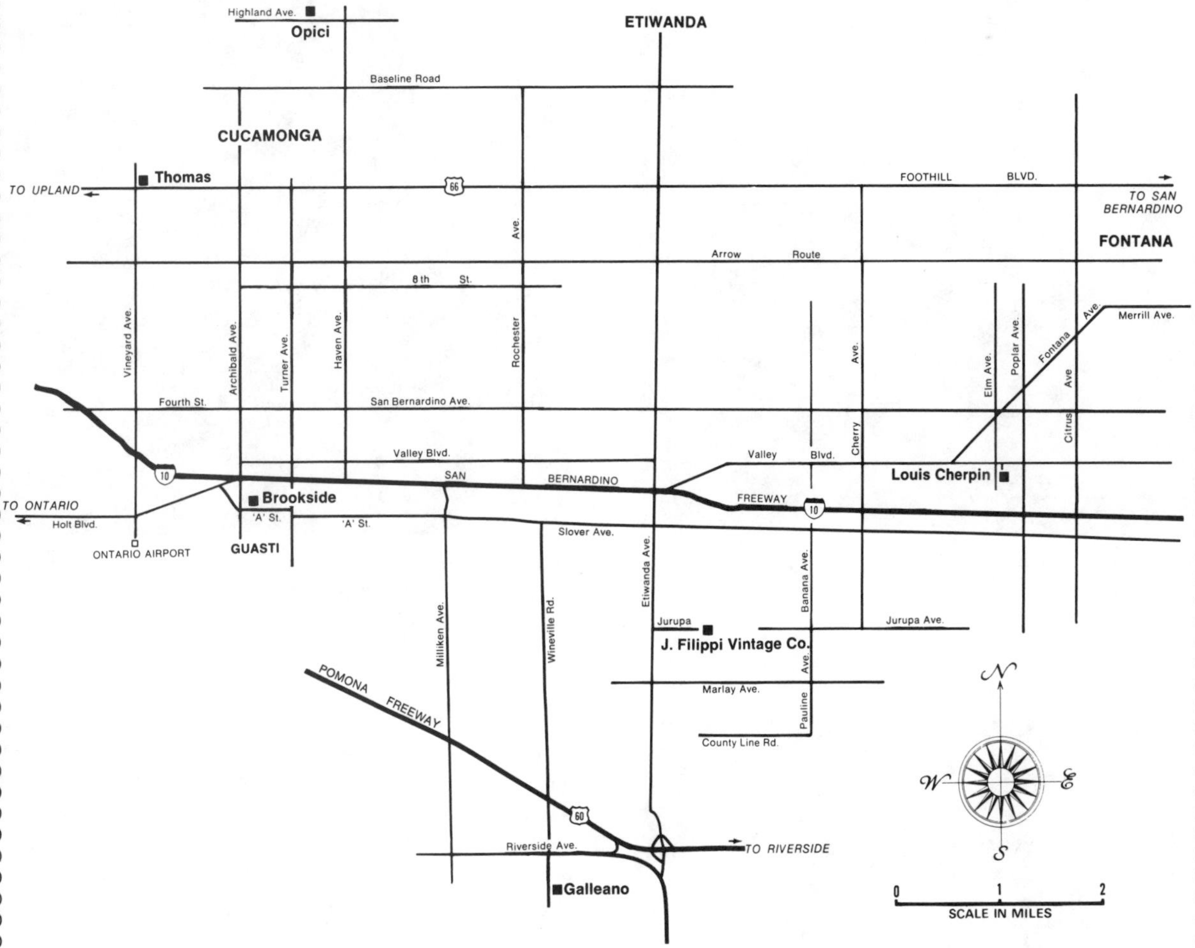
Highland Ave.
Opici
ETIWANDA
Baseline Road
CUCAMONGA
Thomas
TO UPLAND
66
FOOTHILL BLVD.
TO SAN BERNARDINO
FONTANA
Ave.
Arrow Route
8th St.
Merrill Ave.
Fontana Ave.
Vineyard Ave.
Archibald Ave.
Turner Ave.
Haven Ave.
Rochester
Ave.
Elm Ave.
Poplar Ave.
Ave.
Fourth St.
San Bernardino Ave.
Cherry
Citrus
Valley Blvd.
Valley Blvd.
Louis Cherpin
10
SAN BERNARDINO FREEWAY
TO ONTARIO
Brookside
Holt Blvd.
'A' St.
'A' St.
Slover Ave.
ONTARIO AIRPORT
GUASTI
Etiwanda Ave.
Banana Ave.
Milliken Ave.
Wineville Rd.
Jurupa
J. Filippi Vintage Co.
Jurupa Ave.
Ave.
POMONA FREEWAY
Marlay Ave.
Pauline
County Line Rd.
N
W
E
S
60
Riverside Ave.
TO RIVERSIDE
Galleano
0 1 2
SCALE IN MILES

CUCAMONGA DISTRICT

BROOKSIDE. From San Bernardino Fwy (I 10), Archibald Ave. exit, S 2 blks to A St. (9900 A St., Guasti 91743. Tel [714] 983-2787) Picnic. Daily, 8-6. IT weekdays, GT weekends/Ta

L. CHERPIN WINERY. From San Bernardino Fwy., Citrus Ave. exit, N to Valley Blvd., then W ¾ mi. to winery drive S side of rd. (15567 Valley Blvd. Fontana 92335. Tel [714] 822-4103) Daily, 8-5. Ta

J. FILIPPI. From San Bernardino Fwy., Etiwanda Ave. exit, S 1 mi. to Jurupa Ave., the winery drive. (PO Box 2, Mira Loma 91752. Tel [714] 984-4514) Picnic. Daily, 8-6. Tour by appt./Ta

GALLEANO WINERY. From U.S. 60, Etiwanda Ave. exit S to Riverside Ave.; W to Wineville Rd.; S to winery. (4231 Wineville Rd., Mira Loma 91752. Tel [714] 685-5376) M-Sa, 9-5. Ta

OPICI. From Foothill Blvd., N 2 mi. on Haven Ave. (or from San Bernardino Fwy., N 4 mi. on Haven Ave.), W ½ mi. on Highland Ave. (10150 Highland Ave., Alta Loma 91701. Tel [714] 987-2710) Th-M, 10-6, Ta

THOMAS. NE corner of Foothill Blvd. at Vineyard Ave. (8916 Foothill Blvd., Cucamonga 91730. Tel [714] 987-1612) Picnic. Daily, 8-6. IT/Ta

WINERIES OUTSIDE OF MAP AREA

SAN ANTONIO (Los Angeles). From City Hall in downtown Los Angeles, NE 1½ mi. on N. Main St. to Lamar St., S to winery. (737 Lamar St., Los Angeles 90031. Tel [213] 223-1401) Picnic, by res. Daily, 8-8. GT/Ta

CALLAWAY VINEYARDS & WINERY (Rancho California). From U.S. 395 Temecula exit E. 4 mi. via Rancho California Rd. (PO Box 275, Temecula 92390. Tel [714] 676-5283) Visit by appt.

KEY: *GT (guided tour); IT (informal tour); Ta (tasting).*

GHOST OF GARRETT — former winery building now provides background for hip moviemakers.

WATERWHEEL WORKED pumps at Thomas winery for years, now serves only to charm visitors of all ages.

AFTER BARREL AGING, Zinfandel is bottled by automatic filler at J. Filippi winery near Fontana.

Boulevard. The retail room in a small frame building faces the winery door. In it, the Cherpins offer half-gallon and gallon jugs of table wines under the family name. They have another line of table wines in fifths, called *Pour le Gourmet* in tribute to the family's French origins. Several dessert wines round out the list.

J. Filippi Vintage Company, on the edge of Fontana and at the end of a row of industrial concerns, encourages its visitors to limit their inspection of the premises to the tasting room, which is comfortably airy.

The rest of the winery is darker and more constricted. It gives the impression of aged buildings (they date from 1934) and random design. But there are up-to-date features, including stainless steel fermentors, a modern bottling line, and the most modern of filters.

On hand for tasting are a number of table, sparkling, and dessert wines. The varietal table wines are produced elsewhere. The numerous generic types are made here, as are several dessert wines, including one called Marsovo, which has as one ingredient a trace of egg. The labels are Joseph Filippi and Chateau Filippi.

The winery and adjacent family home are surrounded by an expansive vineyard, all well trained and much of it newly planted in 1967. It makes a startling contrast to the dead and abandoned vines across Etiwanda Avenue and elsewhere in the immediate neighborhood.

The Filippi family maintains several tasting rooms elsewhere in Southern California. They will send a list of addresses on request.

Galleano Winery, after years of shy withdrawal from public attention, opened a tasting room in the early 1970s.

The winery, founded by Domenic Galleano in 1933, continues in family hands. It is, by a very narrow margin, in Riverside County rather than San Bernardino.

Wines under the Galleano label are generics save for Zinfandel. They all are on hand for tasting in a gracious but highly informal atmosphere.

The tasting room is housed in a modest frame building at the rear of a courtyard formed by equipment barns, a few yards off the narrow, bumpy surface of Wineville Road. A pleasing collection of old wood tanks is sheltered within a building that shows each of its several expansions through changes in wall material. It still is too small to require a tour.

Opici Winery has a building open to the public tucked away at the end of a street next to a platoon of Alta Loma tract homes. The square, flat-roofed, cream-colored building, on neatly landscaped grounds, has no mechanical parts in plain view.

The wines, in a traditionally appointed tasting room and retail outlet, include, as part of a wide range of varietal table wines, two local Zinfandels (one with a conventional label and the other identifiable by a sultry lady printed in four colors) and Barbera (conventional label). The varietal wines are supplemented by pink and white carbonated wines and several generics, all labeled Opici.

Thomas Vineyards in Cucamonga is one claimant of the title of California's oldest winery. Technicalities of the claim aside, the west end of the building is very old and pleasing to the eye. It is of adobe and dates back to 1839. (Though the east end is quite new, it is a faithful restoration of the original; a flood washed that end away in 1969.)

The wines, labeled Thomas Vineyard and Old Rancho, are available for tasting and sale only on the premises. Along with sales, the proprietors allow visitors to wander around the aging cellars and the grounds. Thomas continues as a working winery, but some of the parts are kept around merely as exhibits in an informal museum of winemaking.

Other Than Wineries

The most notable tourist attractions other than wineries in this region are shoreside parks at reservoirs well up into the San Gabriel Mountains — too distant to lend themselves to inclusion in a day of winery touring. But a couple of local picnic parks add greatly to the opportunities offered by the wineries themselves.

Upland-Cucamonga Regional Park, operated by San Bernardino County, has picnic facilities, children's playgrounds, a swimming lagoon, and a couple of fishing ponds. The park is on Archibald Avenue just a few yards north of the interchange on Interstate 10. There is a minimal day-use fee.

PLAN A GRAND PICNIC

Of the numerous kinds of picnics to take to the wine country, a box dinner is especially practical and can be quite elegant. It is easily transported to a picnic spot. If you run short of time or the weather doesn't cooperate, the picnic can be served in the car.

Pack one box per person with a brightly colored paper place mat and matching napkin, along with a wine glass, fork and spoon, small shaker of salt, and a packet of chemically treated papers to wash sticky fingers.

The menu given here can be made and refrigerated a day ahead, assembled and quickly boxed on the day of the picnic.

Salted nuts

*Cold roasted game hen (one per person)
garnished with
carrot sticks, cherry tomatoes, and raw cauliflower
cut in thick slices*

Poached asparagus spears to dip in Béarnaise sauce

Egg twist bread and butter sandwiches

Rum Baba (homemade or canned)

Fresh pear   Port Salut cheese

After-dinner mints

Wine selected on your taste-tour

Vacuum bottle of coffee or tea

Small pieces of disjointed roasted Cornish game hen are just the right size for eating with your fingers. Package game hen in foil, paper, or plastic dish with the poached asparagus spears and raw vegetables. Be sure container holding Béarnaise sauce has securely fitted lid. Cut the bread and butter sandwiches in halves and allow about three portions for each person.

OUTSTRETCHED PALM tries to appear at ease amid endless rows of vines surrounding it near Mira Loma.

Upland Memorial Park, spacious and shady, offers a considerable number of picnic tables to supplement the ones at the wineries. The town baseball diamond is adjacent. Since this is Southern California, there are weekend games the year around. Any Sunday afternoon, even in February, the temperature might reach 80°.

The park flanks Foothill Boulevard toward the east side of town.

Plotting a Route

Ontario and Upland run into one another so smoothly that the change is imperceptible to all but devoted readers of roadside signs. Together, the towns straddle every major east-west road between Los Angeles and the state line. For visitors to wineries, the most useful of these are Interstate 10, the San Bernardino freeway, and Foothill Boulevard, a moderately fast, four-lane commercial road that once was part of the much sung-about Route 66.

The whole district is divided into a tidy gridwork of local roads. The most useful of the north-south arteries are Vineyard, Archibald, and Etiwanda avenues.

LOS ANGELES CITY AND COUNTY

Early in the history of wine in California, a sizable vineyard grew where Union Station now stands. Times have moved so far that now even the railroad station is on its way to being a part of the local past.

The county hardly can be called "Wine Country" in any general sense. In most years San Antonio Winery can advertise itself as the only producing winery within the city limits of Los Angeles, though a few small firms have come and gone in the recent past. The grapes that supply San Antonio (and the others) tend to come from afar.

San Antonio Winery perseveres as a producing winery, in spite of its downtown Los Angeles location. From the front, on Lamar Street, it is not notably picturesque. Cask heads mounted alongside the door save it from being one more warehouse in a row of them. Inside, though, there is enough old oak cooperage to set a mood. Even more surprising on the premises is a picnic ground big enough to accommodate 100; reservations are necessary for small groups or large.

The Ribolis, the present owners, who are related to founder Santo Cambianica, will take visitors on a winery tour to see the crusher, press, fermenting room, aging cellars, and bottling lines. An appointment is needed for the full-fledged tour, but casual visitors can poke around within limits.

In the tasting room, visitors can assess an extensive line of mellow table wines and two even more extensive lines of dry wines (one local and one from Sonoma). The mellow wines are all generics; the Hillside dry wines are mostly generics and the others mostly varietal. The San Antonio label also offers a complete list of appetizer and dessert types and 15 different sparkling wines. All but the sparkling wines are available for tasting.

San Antonio maintains other tasting rooms scattered across Southern California.

Index to Wineries and the Wine Country

(Boldface numerals indicate map pages)

Photographers

Nancy Anderson: 48 (top). **Ernest Braun:** 10 (top right), 106 (left). **Glenn Christiansen:** 22, 23, 50 (center), 60 (center), 65 (left and center), 86 (right), 94 (top right), 102, 109. **Frances Coleberd:** 29, 74. **Ken Cooperrider:** 60 (left). **Richard Dawson, Jr.:** 72 (bottom). **Richard Dawson, Sr.:** 48 (bottom), 54 (right). **Lee Foster:** 45. **Mike Hayden:** 16 (center). **Elizabeth Hogan:** 90. **Blair Horne:** 10 (left), 14, 19 (top), 33 (bottom), 46 (right), 50 (left and top right), 52, 56. **Walter Houk:** 104 (top right). **Verna R. Johnson:** 94 (center). **Jim Martin:** 88. **Ells Marugg:** 16 (top). **Jack McDowell:** 91 (left). **Joe Munroe:** 28 (center), 61, 62, 95. **Ralph Poole:** 104 (left). **Pete Redpath:** 68 (left). **Schramsberg:** 42 (left). **Simi Winery:** 20. **Eugene Stein:** 108 (right). **Ted Streshinsky:** 60 (top right), 75, 76, 78, 79. **Sunset Staff:** 89. **Bob Thompson:** 18 (right), 19 (bottom), 28 (right top and bottom), 34, 36, 37, 39, 41, 42 (right), 43, 46 (left), 47, 54 (left), 69, 72 (top), 82 (center), 87, 94 (bottom right), 100, 101, 103, 104 (center and bottom right), 110. **Harolyn Thompson:** 10 (bottom right), 24, 32 (bottom), 40, 44, 49 (bottom), 64, 67, 73, 84, 91 (right), 92, 96, 108 (top left). **Mike Tilden:** 68 (right). **Craig Vetter:** 49 (top). **Darrow M. Watt:** 16 (bottom), 18 (left), 26, 82 (right). **Wine Institute:** 6, 7, 11, 12 (left), 28 (left), 32 (top), 33 (top), 50 (bottom right), 51, 60 (bottom right), 65 (right), 66, 82 (left and bottom), 83, 86 (left), 94 (left), 105, 106 (right), 108 (bottom). **George Woo:** 38.